T. LOBSANG RAMPA

Living With The Lama

Special Reprint by
**INNER LIGHT
PUBLICATIONS**

Living With the Lama

ISBN: 1892062399

T. Lobsang Rampa

Books by T. Lobsang Rampa

THE THIRD EYE
DOCTOR FROM LHASA
THE RAMPA STORY
THE CAVE OF THE ANCIENTS
LIVING WITH THE LAMA
YOU FOREVER
WISDOM OF THE ANCIENTS
THE SAFFRON ROBE
CHAPTERS OF LIFE
THE HERMIT
FEEDING THE FLAME
THE THIRTEENTH CANDLE
CANDLELIGHT
AS IT WAS
TWILIGHT
I BELIEVE
THREE LIVES
BEYOND THE TENTH
TIBETAN SAGE

****

THE RAMPA STORY

LIVING WITH THE LAMA

25 years with lobsang rampa

CONTENTS

Living with the Lama

Foreword

"You've gone off your head, Feef," said the Lama. "Who will believe that YOU wrote a book?" He smiled down at me and rubbed under my chin in just the way I liked best before he left the room on some business.

I sat and pondered. "Why should I not write a book?" I thought. True that I am a Cat, but not an ordinary cat.

Oh dear! No! I am a Siamese Cat who has traveled far and seen much. "Seen?" Well, of course, I am quite blind now, and have to rely on the Lama and the Lady Ku'ei to tell me of the present scene, but I have my memories!

Of course I am old, very old indeed, and not a little infirm, but is that not good reason why I should put on paper the events of my life, while I am able? Here, then, is my version of Living with the Lama, and the happiest days of my life; days of sunshine after a lifetime of shadows.

(Mrs.) Fifi Greywhiskers.

Living with the Lama

Chapter One

Mother-to-Be was shrieking her head off. "I want a Tom," she yelled, "A nice STRONG Tom!" The noise, the People said, was TERRIBLE. But then, Mother was renowned for her loud calling voice. At her insistent demand, all the best catteries in Paris were combed for a suitable Siamese Tom with the necessary pedigree. Shriller and louder grew Mother-to-Be's voice. More and more distraught grew the People as they turned with renewed strength to the search.

At last a very presentable candidate was found and he and Mother-to- Be were formally introduced. From that meeting, in course of time, I appeared, and I alone was allowed to live, my brothers and sisters were drowned.

Mother and I lived with an old French family who had a spacious estate on the outskirts of Paris. The Man was a diplomat of high rank who journeyed to the City most days of the week. Often he would not return at night but would stay in The City with his Mistress. The woman who lived with us, Mme. Diplomat, was a very hard woman, shallow and dissatisfied. We cats were not "Persons" to her (as we are to the Lama) but just things to be shown off at tea parties.

Mother had a glorious figure, with the blackest of black faces and a tail that stood straight up. She had won many many prizes. One day, before I was properly weaned, she sang a song rather more loudly than usual. Mme. Diplomat flew into a tantrum and called the gardener. "Pierre," she shouted, "Take her to the pond instantly, I cannot bear the noise." Pierre, an undersized, sallow faced little Frenchman who hated us because we sometimes helped him with the gardening by inspecting plant roots to see if they were growing, scooped up my beautiful Mother and put her into a dirty old potato sack and marched off into the distance. That night, lonely and afraid, I cried myself to sleep in a cold outhouse where Mme. Diplomat would not be disturbed by my lamentations.

I tossed restlessly, feverishly, on my cold bed of old Paris newspapers thrown on the concrete floor. Pangs of hunger wracked my small frame and I wondered how I would manage.

As the first streaks of dawn reluctantly struggled through the cobweb- covered windows of the outhouse, I started with apprehension as heavy footsteps clattered up the path, hesitated at the door, then pushed it open and entered. "Ah!" I thought in relief, "It is only Madame Albertine, the housekeeper." Creaking and gasping she lowered her massive frame to the floor, dipped a gigantic finger into a bowl of warm milk and gently persuaded me to drink.

For days I walked in the shadow of sorrow, grieving for my murdered Mother, murdered solely because of her glorious singing voice. For days I felt not the warmth of the sun, nor thrilled to the sound of a well-loved voice. I hungered and thirsted, and depended wholly upon the good offices of Madame Albertine. Without her I should have starved to death, for I was then too young to eat unaided.

The days dragged on, and became weeks. I learned to fend for myself, but the hardships of my early life left me with an impaired constitution. The estate was huge, and I often wandered about, keeping away from People, and their clumsy, unguided feet. The trees were my favorites, I climbed them and stretched at length along a friendly bough, basking in the sun. The trees whispered to me, telling me of the happier days to come in the evening of my life. Then I understood them not, but trusted, and kept the words of the trees ever before me, even in the darkest moments.

One morning I awakened with strange, ill-defined longings. I uttered a yelp of interrogation which, unfortunately, Mme. Diplomat heard. "Pierre!" she called, "Fetch a tomcat, any tomcat will do to break her in." Later in the day I was seized and thrown roughly into a wooden box. Almost before I was aware of anyone being present, a disreputable old tomcat leaped upon my back. Mother had had no opportunity to tell me much about the 'facts of life', so I was not prepared for what followed. The battered old tomcat leaped upon me, and I felt a shocking blow. For a moment I thought that one of the People had kicked me.

There was a blinding flash of pain, and I felt something tear. I shrieked in agony and terror and raked fiercely at the old tom ; blood spattered from one of his ears and his yelling voice added to mine. Like a flash of lightning the box top was ripped off and startled eyes peered in. I leaped out; as I escaped I saw the old tom, spitting and snarling, jump straight at Pierre who tumbled over backwards at the feet of Mme. Diplomat.

Streaking across a lawn I made for the shelter of a friendly apple tree. Scrambling up the welcoming trunk, I reached a well-loved limb and lay at full length, panting. The leaves rustled in the breeze and gently caressed me. Branches swayed and creaked and slowly lulled me into the sleep of exhaustion.

For the rest of the day and the whole of the night I lay upon the branch; hungry, afraid and sick, wondering why humans were so savage, so uncaring of the feelings of little animals who were utterly dependent upon them. The night was cold, and a light drizzle blew over from the City of Paris. I was soaked, and shivering, yet was terrified to descend and seek shelter.

The cold light of early morning slowly gave way to the dull grayness of an overcast day. Leaden clouds scudded across the lowering sky. Occasionally there was a spatter of rain.

About mid-morning a familiar figure hove in sight from the direction of the House. Madame Albertine, waddling heavily, and clucking sympathetically, approached the tree, peering short-sightedly. I called weakly to her and she reached her hand towards me. "Ah! My poor little Fifi, come to me quickly for I have your food." I slid backwards along the branch and climbed slowly down the trunk. She knelt in the grass beside me, stroking me as I drank the milk and ate the meat which she had brought. With my meal finished, I rubbed gratefully against her knowing that she did not speak my language, and I did not speak French (although I fully understood it). Lifting me to her broad shoulder, she carried me to the House and took me to her room.

I looked about me in wide-eyed amazement and interest.

This was a new room to me and I thought how very suitable the furnishings would be for stretching one's claws. With me still upon her shoulder, Madame Albertine moved heavily to a wide window seat, and looked out. "Ah!" she exclaimed, exhaling gustily, "The pity of it, amid all this beauty there is so much cruelty." She lifted me to her very ample lap and gazed into my face as she said, "My poor, beautiful little Fifi, Mme. Diplomat is a hard and cruel woman. A social climber if ever there was one. To her you are just a toy to be shown off. To me you are one of the Good God's own creatures. But you will not understand what I am saying, little cat!" I purred to show that I did, and licked her hands. She patted me and said, "Oh! Such love and affection going to waste. You will make a good mother, little Fifi."

As I curled more comfortably on her lap I glanced out of the window. The view was so interesting that I had to get up and press my nose to the glass in order to obtain a better view. Madame Albertine smiled fondly at me as she playfully pulled my tail, but the view engaged my whole attention. She turned and rolled to her knees with a thud. Together we looked out of the window, cheek to cheek.

Below us the well-kept lawns looked like a smooth green carpet fringed by an avenue of stately poplar trees. Curving gently towards the left the smooth grayness of the Drive stretched away to the distant road from whence came the muted roar of traffic surging to and from the great Metropolis. My old friend the Apple Tree stood lonely and erect by the side of a small artificial lake, the surface of which, reflecting the dull grayness of the sky, took upon itself the sheen of old lead. Around the water's edge a sparse fringe of reeds grew, reminding me of the fringe of hair on the head of the old Cur. who came to see "le Duc" -- Mme. Diplomat's husband.

I gazed again at the Pond; and thought of my poor Mother who had been done to death there. "And how many others?" I wondered. Madame Albertine looked suddenly at me and said, "Why, my little Fifi, you are crying I think--yes, you have shed a tear. It is a cruel, cruel world, little Fifi, cruel for all of us." Suddenly, in the distance, little black specks which I knew to be cars turned into the Drive and came speeding up to the house to halt in a flurry of dust and a squeal of tires.

A bell jangled furiously, causing my fur to stand up and my tail to fluff. Madame picked up a black thing which I knew was called a telephone, and I heard Mme. Diplomat's shrill voice pouring agitatedly from it: "Albertine, Albertine, why do you not attend to your duties? Why do I pay you? I am so charitable that I keep you. Come instantly, for we have visitors. You must not laze so Albertine!" The Voice clicked off, and Madame Albertine sighed with Frustration. "Ah! That the war has brought me to this. Now I work for sixteen hours a day for a mere pittance. You rest, little Fifi, and here is a box of earth." Sighing again, she patted me once more and walked out of the room. I heard the stairs creaking beneath her weight, then--silence.

The stone terrace beneath my window was swarming with people. Mme. Diplomat was bowing and being so subservient that I knew there were important persons. Little tables appeared as if by magic, were covered with fine white cloths (I used newspapers -- Le Paris Soir -- as MY tablecloth) and servants carried out food and drink in ample profusion. I turned away to curl up when a sudden thought made my tail fluff in alarm. I had overlooked the most elementary precaution; I had forgotten the first thing my Mother taught me. "ALWAYS investigate a strange room, Fifi," she had said. "Go over everything thoroughly. Check all escape routes. Be wary of the unusual, the unexpected. Never NEVER rest until you know the room!"

Guiltily I rose to my feet, sniffed the air, and decided how to proceed. I would take the left wall first and work my way round. Dropping to the floor I peered beneath the window seat, sniffing for anything unusual. Getting to know the layout, the dangers and the advantages. The wallpaper was flowery and faded. Big yellow flowers on a purple background. Tall chairs, spotlessly clean but with the red velvet seating faded. The undersides of the chairs and tables were clean and free from cobwebs. Cats, you know, see the UNDERSIDE of things, not the top, and humans would not recognize things from our view-point.

A tallboy stood against one wall and I edged into the center of the room so as to decide how to get to the top. A quick calculation showed me that I could leap from a chair to the table -- Oh! How slippery it was! -- and reach the top of the tallboy. For a time I sat there, washing my face and ears as I thought things over. Casually I glanced behind me and almost fell over in startled alarm; a Siamese cat was looking at me -- evidently I had disturbed her while she was washing.

"Strange," I thought, "I did not expect to find a cat here. Madame Albertine must be keeping it secret. I will just say 'hello' " I moved towards her, and she, seemingly having the same idea, moved to me. We stopped with some sort of a window between us. "Remarkable!" I mused, "How can this be?" Cautiously, anticipating a trick, I peered around the back of the window. There was no one there. Amazingly, every move I made she copied. At last it dawned upon me. This was a Mirror, a strange device Mother had told me about. Certainly it was the first I had seen because this was my first visit inside the House. Mme. Diplomat was VERY particular, and cats were not permitted inside the house unless she wanted to show us off -- I so far had been spared that indignity.

"Still," I muttered to myself, "I must get on with my investigation. The Mirror can wait." Across the room I saw a large metal structure with brass knobs at each corner, and the whole space between the knobs covered in cloth. Hastily I leaped from the tallboy to the table -- skidding a little on the high polish -- and jumped straight on to the cloth covered metal structure. I landed in the middle and to my horror the thing threw me up into the air! As I landed again I started to run while I decided what to do next.

For a few moments I sat in the center of the carpet, a red and blue "swirly" design which, although spotlessly clean, had seen much better days elsewhere. It appeared to be just right for stretching claws, so I gave a few tentative tugs at it and it seemed to help me to think more clearly. OF COURSE! That huge structure was a bed. My bed was of old newspapers thrown on the concrete floor of an outhouse; Madame Albertine had some old cloth thrown over a sort of iron frame. Purring with pleasure that I had solved the mysterious matter, I walked toward it and examined the underside with vast interest. Immense springs, covered by what was obviously a tremendous sack, or split sack, bore the weight of the clothes piled upon it. I could clearly discern where Madame Albertine's heavy body had distorted some of the springs and caused them to sag.

In a spirit of scientific investigation I poked at a hanging corner of striped material at the far side near the wall. To my incredulous horror, FEATHERS fluttered out. "Great Tomcats!" I exclaimed, "She keeps DEAD BIRDS here.

No wonder she is so big -- she must eat them in the night." A few more cursory sniffs around, and I had exhausted all the possibilities of the bed.

Peering around, wondering where to look next, I saw an open door. Half a dozen leaps, and I cautiously crouched by a door post and edged forward so that one eye could get a first glimpse. At first sight the picture was so strange that I could not comprehend what I was seeing. Shiny stuff on the floor in a black and white pattern. Against one wall an immense horse trough (I knew about them, we had them near the stables!), while against another wall, on a wooden platform, was the largest porcelain cup that I had ever imagined.

It rested on the wooden platform and had a white wooden lid. My eyes grew rounder and rounder and I had to sit and scratch my right ear while I thought it over. WHO would drink out of a thing this size, I wondered.

Just then I heard the sound of Madame Albertine climbing the creaking stairs. Barely stopping to see that my vibrassae was brushed back tidily, I rushed to the door to greet her. At my shouts of joy she beamed and said, "Ah! Little Fifi, I have robbed the best from the table for you. The cream, and the best of the frog legs, they are for you. Those pigs are stuffing away, FAUGH! They make me sick!" Stooping, she placed the dishes -- REAL dishes! -- right in front of me. But I had no time for food yet, I had to tell her how much I loved her.

I roared with purrs as she swept me up to her ample bosom. That night I slept at the foot of Madame Albertine's bed. Snuggled up on the immense coverlet I was more comfortable than at any time since my Mother was taken from me. My education raced ahead; I discovered the purpose of the "horse trough" and that which in my ignorance I had thought to be a giant porcelain cup. It made me blush all over my face and neck to think how ignorant I had been.

In the morning Madame Albertine dressed and went down the stairs. There came the sounds of much commotion, many loud voices. From the window I saw Gaston the chauffeur putting a high polish on the big Renault car. Then he disappeared, to return shortly dressed in his best uniform. He drove up to the front entrance and servants loaded the luggage space with many cases and bundles. I crouched lower; "Monsieur le Duc" and Mme. Diplomat went to the car, entered, and were driven down the Drive by Gaston.

The noise below me increased, but this time the sound was as of people celebrating. Madame Albertine came creaking and wheezing up the stairs, her face flushed with happiness and wine. "They have gone, Little Fifi," she yelled, apparently thinking that I was deaf; "They have GONE -- for a whole week we are free from their tyranny. Now we have fun!" Grasping me to her, she carried me down the stairs where a party was in progress. The servants all looked happier now, and I felt very proud that Madame Albertine was carrying me, although I feared that my weight of four pounds might tire her.

For a week we all purred together. At the end of that week we straightened the place and put on our most miserable expression in preparation for the return of Mme. Diplomat and her husband. We did not bother at all about him, he usually walked around fingering the Legion of Honor button in his coat lapel. Anyway, he was always thinking of the " Service" and Countries, not of servants and cats. Mme. Diplomat was the trouble, she was a virago indeed, and it was like a reprieve from the guillotine when we heard, on the Saturday, that they would be away for another week or two as they were meeting "The Best People."

Time sped on. In the mornings I would help the gardeners by turning up a plant or two so that I might see if the roots were growing satisfactorily. In the afternoons I would retire to a comfortable branch on the old Apple Tree and dream of warmer climates and age-old temples where the yellow-robed priests moved silently around in pursuit of their religious offices. Then I would awaken suddenly to the sound of airplanes of the French Air Force roaring insanely across the sky.

I was becoming heavy, now, and my kittens were beginning to stir within me. Movement was not so easy, I had to pick my steps. For some days past I had been in the habit of going to the Dairy and watching the milk from the cows being put into a thing which whirred and produced two streams, one of milk and one of cream. I sat upon a low shelf, out of everyone's way. The dairy maid would talk to me and I would answer her.

One evening I was sitting on the shelf, about six feet from a half full churn of milk. The dairymaid was talking to me about her latest boy friend and I was purring to her, assuring her that everything would be all right between them. Suddenly there was an ear-splitting shriek, like a Tom with his tail stepped on. Mme. Diplomat rushed into the Dairy shouting, "I told you not to have cats in here, you will POISON us!" She picked up the first thing to hand, a copper measure, and flung it with all her strength at me. It caught me in the side most violently and knocked me of into the milk churn. The pain was terrible. I could hardly paddle to keep afloat. I felt my insides oozing out. The floor shook under heavy footsteps, and Madame Albertine appeared.

Quickly she tipped the churn and poured out the blood-stained milk. Gently she placed her hands upon me. "Call Mister the Veterinarian," she commanded. I swooned off. When I awakened I was in Madame Albertine's bedroom, in a warmly-lined box. Three ribs were broken, and I had lost my kittens. For a time I was very ill indeed. Mister the Veterinarian came to see me often and I was told that he had said stern words to Mme. Diplomat. "Cruelty. Needless cruelty," he had said. "People will not like it. People will say that you are a bad woman. The servants told me," he said, "That the little mother cat was very clean and VERY honest. No, Mme. Diplomat, it was very bad of you."

Madame Albertine wet my lips with water, for I would turn pale at the thought of milk. Day after day she tried to persuade me to eat. Mister the Veterinarian said, "There is no hope now, she will die, she cannot live another day without food." I lapsed into a coma. From somewhere I seemed to hear the rustling of the trees, the creaking of branches.

"Little Cat," said the Apple Tree, "Little Cat, this is not the end. Do you remember what I told you, Little Cat." Strange noises buzzed in my head.

I saw a bright yellow light, saw wondrous pictures and smelled the pleasures of Heaven.

"Little Cat," whispered the trees, "This is not the end. Eat, and Live. Eat and Live. This is not the end. You have a purpose in life, Little Cat. You shall end your days in joy, in the fullness of years. Not now. This is not the end"

Wearily I opened my eyes and raised my head a trifle. Madame Albertine, with great tears streaming down her cheeks, knelt beside me, holding some finely sliced pieces of chicken. Mister the Veterinarian stood at a table filling a syringe from a bottle. Weakly I took a piece of chicken, held it in my mouth a moment, and swallowed it. "A Miracle! A Miracle!" said Madame Albertine.

Mister the Veterinarian turned, mouth agape, slowly put down the syringe and walked across to me. "It is, as you say, a miracle," he remarked. "I was filling the syringe in order to administer the coup de grace and thus save her any further suffering." I smiled up at them and gave three beats of purr -- all that I could manage. As I slipped again into sleep I heard him say "She will recover."

For a week I was in a sorry state; I could not take a deep breath, nor could I manage more than a few steps. Madame Albertine had brought my earth box very close, for Mother had taught me to be scrupulously careful in my habits.

About a week later, Madame Albertine carried me downstairs. Mme. Diplomat was standing at the entrance to a room looking stern and disapproving. "She must be taken to an outhouse, Albertine," said Mme. Diplomat. "Begging your pardon, Ma'am," said Madame Albertine, "She is not yet well enough, and if she is badly treated I and other servants will leave." With a haughty sniff and stare, Mme. Diplomat turned on her heel and re-entered the room. In the kitchens, 'below stairs,' some of the older women came to speak to me and told me they were glad I looked better.

Madame Albertine gently put me on the floor so that I could move around and read all the news of things and people. I soon tired, for I was as yet far from well, and I went to Madame Albertine, looked up at her face, and told her I wanted to go to bed. She picked me up and carried me to the top of the house again. I was so tired that I was sound asleep before she laid me in my bed.

Chapter Two

It is easy to be wise after the event. Writing a book brings back one's memories. Through years of hardship I often thought of the words of the Old Apple Tree: "Little Cat, this is not the end. You have a purpose in life." Then I thought it was mainly a kindness to cheer me. Now I know better.

Now -- in the evening of my life -- I have much happiness; if I am absent for even a few moments I hear, "Where's Feef? Is she all right?" and I know that I am truly wanted for myself, not just for my appearance. In my young days it was different; I was merely a showpiece, or as modern people have it--a "conversation piece." The Americans would call it a gimmick.

Mme. Diplomat had two obsessions. She was obsessed with the idea that she should climb higher and ever higher in the social scale of France, and showing me off to people was a sure charm to success. It amazed me, because she hated cats (except in public), and I was not allowed in the house unless there were visitors. The memory of the first "show off" is vivid in my mind.

I was in the garden on a warm, sunny day. For some time I had been studying the flowers, watching the bees carry pollen on their legs. Then I moved on to examine the foot of a poplar tree. A neighbor's dog had recently been there and left a message which I wanted to read. Casting frequent glances over my shoulder to see that all was safe, I devoted my attention to the message. Gradually I became more and more interested and more and more withdrawn from the events around me. Unexpectedly, rough hands grabbed me and woke me from my contemplation of the dog-message.

"Pssst!" I hissed as I leaped free, giving a backwards swipe as I did so. Quickly I scrambled up the tree trunk and looked down. "Always run first and look afterwards," Mother had said, "It is better to run needlessly than to stop and never be able to run again."

I looked down. There was Pierre the Gardener holding the end of his nose. A trickle of scarlet blood was leaking past his fingers. Looking at me with hate, he stooped, picked up a stone, and threw it with all his strength. .I dodged round the trunk, but even so the vibration of the stone against the trunk almost shook me free. He bent to pick up another stone just as the bushes parted behind him and Madame Albertine, walking silently on the mossy ground, stepped through.

Taking in the scene at a glance, she swiftly shot a foot forward, and Pierre fell face-down on to the earth. She grabbed him by his collar and jerked him upright. Shaking him violently -- he was just a little man -- she swung him round.

"You hurt that cat and I KILL you, see! Mme. Diplomat sent you to find her, you son of a pig, not hurt her."

"The cat jumped out of my hands and I fell against the tree and made my nose bleed," Pierre muttered, "I lost my temper because of the pain." Madame Albertine shrugged and turned to me. "Fifi, Fifi, come to Mama," she called.

"I'm coming," I yelled as I put my arms round the tree trunk and slithered down backwards.

"Now you be on your best behavior, Little Fifi," said Madame Albertine, "The Mistress wants to show you to her visitors." The term "Mistress" always amused me. Monsieur le Duc had a Mistress in Paris, so how was Mme. Diplomat the Mistress. However, I thought, if they want her to be called "Mistress" as well it will not hurt me! These were very strange and irrational people.

We walked together across the lawn, Madame Albertine carrying me so that my feet should be clean for the visitors. Up the broad stone steps we went -- I saw a mouse scurry into a hole by a bush -- and across the balcony. Through the open doors of the Salon I saw a crowd of people sitting and chattering like a flock of starlings. "I have brought Fifi, Madame!" said Madame Albertine. "The Mistress" jumped to her feet and gingerly took me from my friend. "Oh my darling sweet little Fifi!" she exclaimed as she turned so quickly that I was made giddy. Women rose to their feet and crowded close, uttering exclamations of delight. Siamese Cats were a rarity in France in those days. Even the men present moved to have a look. My black face and white body, ending with a black tail, seemed to intrigue them. "Rarest of the rare," said the Mistress, "A wonderful pedigree, she cost a fortune. So affectionate, she sleeps with me at night." I yelled a protest at such lies, and everyone jumped back in alarm. "She is only talking," said Madame Albertine, who had been ordered to stay in the Salon "just in case." Like me, Madame Albertine's face was registering astonishment that the Mistress should tell such absolute falsehoods. "Oh, Renee," said a women visitor, "You should take her to America when you go, American women can very greatly assist your husband's career if they like you and the little cat certainly draws attention." The Mistress pursed up her thin lips so that her mouth completely disappeared. "Take her?" she queried, "How would I do that? She would make trouble and then there would be difficulties when we brought her back."

"Nonsense, Renee, I am surprised at you," replied her friend. "I know a vet who can give you a drug to put her to sleep for the whole air trip. You can have her go in a padded box as diplomatic luggage." The Mistress nodded her head, "Yes, Antoinette, I will have that address, please," she answered.

For some time I had to remain in the Salon while people exclaimed at my figure, expressed amazement at the length of my legs and the blackness of my tail. "I thought all the best type of Siamese cat had a kinky tail," said one. "Oh, no," asserted the Mistress, "Siamese cats with kinked tails are not now the fashion. The straighter the tail the better the cat. Shortly we shall send this one to be mated then we shall have kittens for disposal."

At long last Madame Albertine left the Salon. "Phew!" she exclaimed, "Give me four-legged cats any time rather than that two-legged variety." Quickly I glanced around, I had never seen two-legged cats before and did not really understand how they would manage. There was nothing behind me except the closed door so I just shook my head in bewilderment and walked on beside Madame Albertine.

Darkness was falling and a light rain was pattering on the windows when the telephone in Madame Albertilie's room jangled irritably. She rose to answer it and the Mistress's shrill voice disturbed the peace. "Albertine, have you the cat in your room?" "Yes, Ma'am, she is not yet well." replied Madame Albertine. The Mistress's voice rose an octave, "I have told you, Albertine, I will not have her in the house unless visitors are here. Take her to the outhouse at once. I wonder at my goodness in keeping you, you are so useless!"

Reluctantly Madame Albertine drew on a heavy woolen knitted coat, struggled into a raincoat, and wrapped a scarf around her head. Lifting me, she wrapped a shawl around me and carried me down the backstairs. Stopping at the Servants' Hall to pick up a flashlight, she walked to the door. A blustering wind blew into our faces. Scudding clouds raced low across the night sky. From a tall poplar tree an owl hooted dismally as our presence scared off the mouse which he had been hunting. Rainladen branches brushed against us and shed their load of water over us. The path was slippery and treacherous in the dark. Madame Albertine cautiously shuffled along, picking her steps by the feeble light of the flashlight, muttering imprecations against Mme. Diplomat and all she stood for.

The outhouse loomed before us, a darker patch in the darkness of the shading trees. She pushed open the door and entered. There was a frightening crash as a plantpot, caught by her voluminous clothes, swept to the floor. In spite of myself, my tail fluffed with fright and a sharp ridge formed along the length of my spine. Flashing her light in a semi-circle before her, Madame Albertine edged further into the shed toward the pile of old newspapers which was my bed.

"I'd like to see That Woman shut in a place like this," she muttered to herself. "It would knock some of the fancy airs out of her." Gently she put me down, saw that there was water for me -- I never drank milk now, only water -- and put a few scraps of frogs' legs beside me. Patting my head, she slowly backed out and shut the door behind her. The fading sound of her footsteps was drowned by the keening of the wind and the pattering of the rain upon the galvanized iron roof.

I hated this shed. Often people forgot all about me, and I could not get out until the door was opened. All too frequently I stayed there without food or water for two or even three days. Shouts were of no avail, for it was too far from the house, hidden in a grove of trees far at the back of all other buildings. I would just lie and starve, becoming more and more parched, waiting for someone in the house to remember that I had not been seen about for a time, then come and investigate.

Now it is so different; here I am treated as a human. In place of near- starvation I always have food and drink, and I sleep in a bedroom on a real bed of my own. Looking back through the years it seems as if the past was a journey through a long night and I have now emerged into the sunlight and warmth of love. In the past I had to beware of heavy feet.

Now everyone looks out for ME! Furniture is never shifted unless I am made aware of its new location, because I am blind and old and can no longer fend for myself. As the Lama says, I am a dearly loved old granny who is enjoying peace and happiness. As I dictate this I sit in a comfortable chair where the warm rays of the sun fall upon me.

But all things in their place, the Days of Shadows were still upon me and the sunlight had yet to break through the storm-wrack.

Strange stirrings took place within me. Softly, for I was as yet unsure of myself, I sang a song. I padded round the grounds seeking SOMETHING. My longings were vague, yet urgent. Sitting beside an open window -- not daring to enter -- I heard Mme. Diplomat using the telephone. "Yes, she is calling. I will send her immediately and have her collected tomorrow. Yes, I want to sell the kittens as soon as possible." Shortly after, Gaston came to me and put me in a stuffy wooden box with the lid fastened securely. The smell of the box, apart from the stuffiness was MOST interesting.

Groceries had been carried in it. Frogs' legs and snails. Raw meats and things that were green. I was so interested that I hardly noticed when Gaston lifted the box and carried me off to the garage. For a time the box was left resting on the concrete floor. The smell of oil, and petrol made me feel sick. At last Gaston entered the garage again, opened the big front doors, and started up our second car, an old Citroen. Tossing my box rather roughly into the luggage space, he entered the front and drove off. It was a terrible ride, we took corners so fast that my box slid violently and stopped with a bump. At the next corner the process would be repeated. The darkness was intense, and the fumes from the engine exhaust made me choke and cough. I thought the journey would never end.

Violently the car swerved, there was the horrid squeal of skidding rubber, and as the car straightened and shot ahead once more my box rolled over, upside-down. I slid against a sharp splinter and my nose began to bleed. The Citroen shuddered to a stop and soon I heard voices. The luggage compartment was opened and for a moment there was silence, then, "Look, there is blood!" a strange voice said.

My box was lifted, I felt swaying as someone carried it along. Some steps were climbed and shadow fell across the cracks of the box and I guessed that I was inside a house or shed. A door shut, I was lifted higher and put on a table. Fumbling hands scraped against the outer surface, then the lid was thrown open. I blinked in the sudden light.

"Poor little cat!" said a woman's voice. Reaching in she put her hands beneath me and lifted me out. I felt ill, sick and dizzy with the exhaust fumes, half stunned from the violent journey, and bleeding from the nose quite heavily. Gaston stood by looking white and frightened. "I must telephone Mme. Diplomat," said a man. "Don't lose me my job," said Gaston, "I drove very carefully." The man lifted the telephone while the woman mopped the blood from my nose.

"Mme. Diplomat," said the man, "Your little cat is ill, she is underfed and she has been dreadfully shaken by this journey. You will lose your cat, Madame, unless greater care is taken of her."

"Good Gracious me," I heard Mme. Diplomat's voice reply, "Such a trouble for a mere cat. She IS looked after. I do not pamper her and spoil her, I want her to have kittens."

"But Madame," the man replied, "You will have no cat and no kittens if she is treated like this. You -- have a very valuable Pedigree Siamese Cat here, of the best strain in the whole of France. I know, I bred her Mother. To neglect this cat is bad business, like using diamond rings to cut glass."

"I know you," answered Mme. Diplomat, "Is the chauffeur there, I want to speak to him." Silently the man passed the telephone to Gaston. For a time the torrent of words from the

Mistress was so great, so vitriolic, that it defeated its own end and merely bemused the senses. At last, after much haggling, terms were agreed upon. I was to stay at -- where was I?

-- until I was better. Gaston departed, still shivering as he thought of Mme. Diplomat. I lay upon the table as the man and woman worked upon me. There was the sensation of just a little prick and almost before I realized it I was asleep. It was a most peculiar sensation. I dreamed that I was in Heaven and a lot of cats were talking to me, asking where I came from, what I was doing, and who my parents were. They were speaking in best Siamese Cat French, too! Wearily I raised my head and opened my eyes. Surprise at my surroundings caused my tail to fluff and a ridge to form along the length of my spine. Inches from my face was a wire mesh door. I was lying on clean straw. Beyond the wire mesh door was a large room containing all kinds of cats and a few small dogs. My neighbors on each side were Siamese cats.

"Ah! The wreckage is stirring!" said one. "My! Your tail did droop when you were carried in," said the other. "Where did you come from?" yelled a Persian from the opposite side of the room. "These cats make me sick," growled a Toy Poodle from a box on the floor. "Yeh," muttered a small dog just out of my line of sight, "Dese dames would get slapped down real good Stateside." "Hark at that Yank dog shootin' the breeze!" said someone nearby; "He hasn't been here long enough to have a right to talk. Just a boarder, that's what he is!"

"I'm Ghawa," said the cat on my right, "I've been spayed." "Me, I'm Song Tu," said the cat on my left; "I fought with a dog, gee, you should see that dog, I REALLY worked him over!"

"I'm Fifi," I responded timidly, "I didn't know there were any more Siamese cats than my late Mother and me." For a time there was quiet in the big room, then complete uproar broke out as a man entered bearing food. Everyone talked at once. Dogs demanding to be fed first, cats calling the dogs selfish pigs, the clatter of feeding dishes and the gurgle of water as drinking containers were filled. Then the slurp slurp as the dogs started eating.

The man came over and looked at me. The woman entered and came across. "She is awake," said the man. "Nice little cat," said the woman. "We shall have to build her up, she will not have kittens in her present state." They brought me a plentiful supply of food, and moved on to others. I was not feeling so good, but thought it would be bad manners not to eat; so I set to and soon cleared up the whole lot. "Ah!" said the man, coming back, "She was starving." "Let us put her in the Annexe," said the woman, "She will get more sunlight there, I think all these other animals bother her."

The man opened my box and cradled me in his arms as he carried me across the room and through a door which I had not been able to see before. "Goodbye," yelled Ghawa.

"Nice meeting you," screamed Song Tu, "Remember me to the Toms when you meet them!" We passed through the doorway and entered a sunlit room where there was one large cage in the center. "Going to put her in the monkey cage, Boss?" asked a man whom I had not seen before.

"Yes," replied the man who was carrying me, "She needs looking after because she would not carry in her present state." Carry? CARRY? What was I supposed to carry?

Did they think I was going to work here at carrying dishes or something? The man opened the door of the big cage and put me in. It was nice, except for the smell of disinfectant. There were tree branches and shelves and a pleasant, straw-lined box in which I could sleep. I wandered around cautiously, for Mother had taught me to most thoroughly investigate any strange place before settling down. A tree branch was inviting, so I did my claws to show that I had settled in. By walking up the branch I found that I could look over a small hedge and see beyond.

There was a very, very large enclosed space, with netting all the way around it and all the way across the top. Small trees and bushes studded the ground. As I watched, a most magnificent Siamese Tom strolled into view. He was a gorgeous figure, long and slim, with heavy shoulders and the blackest of black tails. As he walked slowly across the ground he was singing the latest love song. I listened entranced, but for the moment was too shy to sing back to him. My heart fluttered, and I had the strangest feelings. A deep sigh escaped me as he wandered out of sight.

For a time I sat bemused on the topmost reach of that branch. My tail twitched spasmodically, and my legs trembled so much with emotion that they would scarce support me. What a Tom, what a superb figure! I could well imagine him gracing a Temple in far-off Siam, with yellow-robed priests greeting him as he lazed in the sun. And -- was I mistaken?-- I felt that he had glanced in my direction, knew all about me. My head was awhirl with thoughts of the future. Slowly, shakily, I descended the branch, entered the sleeping box, and lay down to think things over. That night I slept restlessly, the next day the Man said I had a fever through the bad car journey and the exhaust fumes. I knew why I had the fever! His handsome black face and long sweeping tail had haunted my sleeping hours. The Man said I was in poor condition and must rest. For four days I lived in that cage, resting and eating. The next morning I was led to a little house inside the netting enclosure. Settling down, I looked about me and saw that there was a netting wall between my compartment and that of the Handsome Tom. His room was neat, and well kept, his straw was clean, and I saw that his bowl of water had no dust floating on the surface. He was not in then, I guessed that he was in the enclosed garden seeing about the plants.

Sleepily I closed my eyes and dozed off. A hearty voice jerked me awake and I glanced timidly towards the netting wall. "Well!" said the Siamese Tom, "Glad to meet you, I'm sure." His big black face pressed close to the netting, his vivid blue eyes flashing his thoughts towards me. "We are being married this afternoon," he said, "I'll like that, will you?" Blushing all over, I hid my face in the straw. "Oh, don't worry so," he exclaimed, "We are doing noble work, there are not enough of us in France. You'll like it, you'll see!" he laughed as he settled down to rest after his morning walk.

At lunchtime the Man came in and laughed as he found us, sitting close with only the netting between us, singing a duet. The Tom rose to his feet and roared to the Man: "Get this * * * * * door out of the way!" using some words which made me blush all over again. The Man leisurely unlatched the door, hooked it back safely, and turned and left us.

Oh! That Tom, the ardor of his embraces, the things he said to me. Afterwards we lay side by side in a warm glow, and I had the chilling thought; I was not the first! I rose to my feet and strolled back to my own room. The Man came in and once again shut the screen door between us. In the evening he came and carried me back to the big cage. I slept soundly.

In the morning the Woman came and carried me off to the room at which I first entered the building. She put me on a table and held me securely while the Man carefully examined me all over. "I shall have to see this cat's Owner because the Little thing has been badly treated. See - " he said, pointing to my left ribs and pressing where it was still tender, "Something dreadful has happened to her and she is too valuable an animal to be neglected." "Shall we take a ride in that direction tomorrow and have a word with the Owner?" The Woman seemed to be really interested in me. The Man answered, saying, "Yes, we will take her back, we might be able to collect our fees at the same time. I will telephone her and say that we will deliver the cat and collect the money."

He picked up the phone and eventually spoke to Mme. Diplomat. Her sole concern appeared to be that the 'cat delivery' might cost her a few francs more. Assured that it would not, she agreed to pay the bill as soon as I was returned. So it was decided, I should stay until the following afternoon and then should be returned to Mme. Diplomat.

"Here, Georges," called the Man, "Take her back to the monkey cage, she is staying until tomorrow." Georges, an old bent man whom I had not seen before; shambled over to me and lifted me with surprising care. Placing me on his shoulder he walked away. Into the Big Room he carried me, not stopping so that I could have a word with the others. Into the Other Room, where he entered the Monkey Cage and shut the door behind us. For a few short moments he trailed a piece of string in front of me. "Poor little thing," he muttered to himself, "It is clear that no one has ever played with you in your short life!"

Alone once more; I walked up the sloping branch and looked out across the wired enclosure. No emotion stirred within me now, I knew that the Tom had plenty of Queens, and I was just one of a long line. People who know cats always call the males "toms" and the females "queens." It has nothing to do with pedigree, but is just a generic term.

A solitary branch was swaying, bending beneath a considerable weight. As I watched the big Tom sprang from the tree and plummeted to earth. Rushing up the trunk he did the same thing again, and again. I watched in fascination, then it dawned upon me that he was taking his morning exercise! Idly, for want of something better to do, I lay upon my branch and sharpened my claws until they shone like the pearls around Mme. Diplomat's neck. Then, bored, I slept in the comforting warmth of the noonday sun.

Some time later, when the sun was no longer directly overhead but had moved to warm some other part of France, I was awakened by a soft, motherly voice. Peering with some difficulty at a window almost out of my reach, I saw an old black queen, one who had seen many many summers. She was decidedly plump, and as she sat there on the window ledge, washing her ears, I thought how nice it would be to have a chat.

"Ah!" she said, "so you are awake. I hope you are enjoying your stay here; we pride ourselves that we give better service than anywhere else in France. Are you eating well?"

"Yes, thank you," I replied, "I am being looked after very well. Are you Madame the Proprietress?"

"No," she answered, "Although many people think I am. I have the responsible task of teaching new Stud Toms their duties; I give them a tryout before they are put in general circulation. It is very important, very exacting work." We sat for a few moments, absorbed in our own thoughts.

"What is your name?" I asked.

"Butterball," she replied, "I used to be very plump, and my coat used to shine like butter, but that was when I was much younger," she added. "Now I do a variety of tasks --besides THAT which I told you, you know. I also police the food stores to see that the mice do not disturb us." She relaxed into contemplation of her duties, and then said, "Have you tried our raw horsemeat yet? Oh, you simply MUST try it before you leave. It is truly delicious, the best horsemeat you can buy anywhere. I believe that we may be having some for supper, I saw Georges -- that's the helper, you know --cutting it up just a few moments ago." She paused, then said in a satisfied voice, "Yes, I'm SURE there is horsemeat for supper." We sat and thought, and washed a little, then Madame Butterball said, "Well, I must go, I will see that you get a good helping -- I believe I can smell Georges bringing supper now!" She jumped from the window. In the Big Room behind me I could hear shouts and yells. "HORSEMEAT!" "Feed me first!" "I'm starving -- quick, Georges!"

But Georges took no notice, instead he came through the Big Room and straight in to me, serving ME first. "You first, Little Cat," he said. "The others can wait. You are the quietest of the lot, so you get served first." I purred at him to show that I fully appreciated the honor. He put before me a great quantity of meat. It had a wonderful scent. I rubbed against his legs and purred my loudest. "You are only a little cat," he said, "I will cut it up for you." He very civilly cut the whole lot into pieces then, with a "Have a good meal, cat!" he went off to attend to the others.

The meat was just wonderful, sweet to the taste, and tender to the tooth. At long last I sat back and washed my face. A scrabbling sound made me look up just as a black face with twinkling eyes appeared at the window. "Good, wasn't it?" said Mme. Butterball. "What did I tell you? We serve the best horsemeat obtainable here. You wait, though; FISH for breakfast! Lovely stuff, I have just tasted it myself, Oh well, have a good night!" With that she turned and was gone.

Fish? I could not think of food now, I was full. This was such a change from the food at home, there I was given scraps which humans had left, messed up stuff with silly sauces which often burned my tongue. Here rats lived in real French style.

The light was fading as the sun set in the Western sky. Birds came flapping home, old ravens calling to their fellows, discussing the events of the day. Soon the dusk deepened, and bats came fluttering by, their leathery wings creaking as they wheeled and turned in pursuit of night insects. Over the tall poplar trees the orange moon peeped shyly, as if hesitant about intruding upon the darkness of the night. With a sigh of contentment, I climbed lazily into my box and fell asleep.

I dreamed, and all my longings came to the surface. I dreamed that someone wanted me just for myself, just for companionship. My heart was full of love, love which had to be suppressed because no one at my home knew of a little girl cat's longings and desires. Now, as an old woman cat, I am surrounded with love and I give my all in return. We know hardship, now, and shortages, but to me this is THE perfect life, where I am one with the family and loved as a real person.

The night passed. I was restless and ill at ease wondering about going home. Would it be hardship again? Would I have a bed of straw instead of old, damp newspapers? I wondered. The next thing I knew it was daylight. A dog was barking mournfully in the Big Room. "I want out, I want out," he was saying, over and over. "I want out!" Nearby a bird was telling off her mate for being late with the breakfast. Gradually the usual sounds of the day came to life. The bell in a church tower clanged as its brazen voice called the humans to do some sort of service. "After Mass I am going to the town to get a new blouse, will you give me a lift?" asked a female voice. They passed from my hearing before I could catch the man's reply. The clattering of buckets reminded me that it would soon be time for breakfast. From the netted enclosure the Handsome Tom lifted up his voice in a song of praise to greet the new day.

The Woman came with my breakfast. "Hello, cat," she said, "Have a good meal because you are going home this afternoon." I purred and rubbed against her to show that I understood. She was wearing new, frilly underthings, and she appeared to be in the best of spirits. I often smile to myself when I think of how we cats see people! Often we can tell a person's mood by their underclothes. Our viewpoint is different, you see.

The fish was very good, but it was covered with some meal, or wheatey stuff, which I had to scrape off. "Good, isn't it?" said a voice from the window.

"Good morning, Madame Butterball," I replied. "Yes, this is very good, but what is this covering to it?" Madame Butterball laughed good-naturedly. "Oh!" she exclaimed, "You must be a country girl! Here we ALWAYS -- but ALWAYS -- have cereals in the morning so that we get our vitamins." "But why did I not have them before?" I persisted. "Because you were under treatment and had them in liquid form." Madame Butterball sighed, "I must go now, there is always so much to do, and so little time. I will try to see you before you leave." Before I could reply she had jumped off the window, and I could hear her rustling through the bushes.

There was a confused babble of talk from the Big Room. "Yeh," said the American dog, "So I sez to him, I don't want you nosin' around MY lamp post, see! You allus snoops round to see what you can sniff out." Tong Fa, a Siamese Cat who came in late in the evening, was talking to Ghawa. "Tell me, Madame, are we not permitted to investigate the grounds here?" I curled up and had a sleep, all this talk was making my head ache.

"Shall we put her in a basket?" I awoke with a start. The Man and the Woman entered my room by a side door. "Basket?" asked the Woman, "No, SHE does not need putting in a basket, I will have her on my lap." They walked to the window and stood talking. "That Tong Fa," mused the Woman, "It is a shame to put him to sleep. Can't we do something about it" The Man shifted uncomfortably and rubbed his chin. "What CAN we do? The cat is old and nearly blind. The Owner has no time for him. What CAN we do?" There was silence for a long time. "I don't like it," said the Woman, "it's murder!" The Man remained silent.

I made myself as small as possible in a corner of the cage. Old and blind? Was that grounds for a death sentence? No thought for years of devotion and love, kill the Old Ones off if they could not fend for themselves. Together the Man and the Woman walked into the Big Room and gently took old Tong Fa from his cage.

The morning dragged on. I had somber thoughts. What would happen to me when I was old? Apple Tree had told me that I would have happiness, but when one is young and inexperienced waiting seems an age without end. Old Georges came in. "Here is a little horsemeat, small cat. Eat it up because you are going home soon." I purred and rubbed against him, and he stooped to stroke my head. Barely had I finished eating, and doing my toilet, when the Woman came for me. "Here we go, Fifi!" she exclaimed, "Home to Mme. Diplomat (the old witch)." She picked me up and carried me through the side door. Madame Butterball was waiting.

"Goodbye, Feef," she yelled, "Come and see us again soon."

"Goodbye, Madame Butterball," I replied, "Many thanks for your hospitality."

The Woman walked on to where the Man was waiting beside a big old car. She got in, made sure the windows were almost shut, then the Man got in and started the engine. We drove off and turned on to the road leading to my home.

Chapter Three

The car hummed along the highway. Tall poplar trees stood proudly at the side of the road, with frequent gaps in their ranks as testimony to the ravages of a great war, a war which I knew about only by listening to humans. We sped on, seemingly endlessly. Vaguely I wondered how these machines worked, how did they run so fast and so long ? It was but a vagrant thought, my attention was almost wholly held by the sights of the passing countryside.

For the first mile or so I had sat upon the Woman's lap. Curiosity got the better of me, and I walked somewhat unsteadily to the back of the car and sat on a shelf level with the rear window, a shelf where there was a Michelin guide, maps and other things. I could see the road behind us. The Woman moved up close to the Man and they murmured sweet things together. I wondered if she also was going to have kittens.

The sun was an hour across the sky as the Man said, "We should be almost there." "Yes," replied the Woman, "I believe it is the big house a mile and a half beyond the church. We shall soon find it." We drove on more slowly now, slowing to a stop as we turned into the Drive and found the gates shut. A discreet "toot" and a man came running out of the Lodge and approached the car. Seeing and recognizing me, he turned and opened the gates. It gave me quite a thrill to realize that I had been instrumental in having the gates opened without there having to be any explanations given.

We drove on, and the Gatekeeper gravely acknowledged me as we passed. My life had been very narrow, I decided, for I had not even known of the Lodge, or of the gates. Mme. Diplomat was at the side of one of the lawns talking to one of Pierre's helpers. She turned at our approach and walked slowly towards us. The Man stopped the car, got out, and bowed politely to her. "We have brought your little cat, Madame," he said, "and here is a certified copy of the Stud Tom's pedigree." Mme. Diplomat's eyes opened wide when she saw me sitting in the car. "Did you not confine her in a box?" she asked. "No, Madame," replied the Man, "She is a good little cat and she has been quiet and well-behaved all the time she was with us. We consider her to be an exceptionally well-behaved cat." I felt myself blushing at such praise, and I confess that I was unmannerly enough to purr with complete agreement. Mme. Diplomat imperiously turned to the assistant gardener and said, "Run to the House, tell Madame Albertine I want her instantly."

"Yah!" yelled the Lodgekeeper's Tomcat from behind a tree, "I know where you have been! Us Working Toms are not good enough for you, you have to have Fancy Boys!"

"Oh my goodness," said the Woman in the car, "there is a cat. Fifi must be kept from Toms." Mme. Diplomat whirled, and threw a stick which she snatched from the ground. It missed the Lodgekeeper's cat by feet. "Ha! Ha!" he laughed as he ran off, "You couldn't hit a church steeple with a whisk-broom if you were six inches from it, you * * * * * old woman!" I blushed again. The language was terrible, and I felt a deep sense of relief as I saw Madame Albertine waddling down the Drive at top speed, her face radiant with welcome.

I yelled at her and jumped straight into her arms, telling her how much I loved her, how I had missed her, and all that had happened to me. For a time we were oblivious to everything except each other, then Mme. Diplomat's rasping voice jerked us back to the present. "ALBERTINE!" she grated, "Are you aware that I am addressing you? Pay attention immediately."

"Madame," said the Man who had driven me, "This cat has been neglected. She has not had enough to eat. Scraps are NOT good enough for Pedigree Siamese Cats, and they should have a warm, comfortable bed. This cat is VALUABLE," he went on, "and would be a show-cat if she were better looked after."

Mme. Diplomat fixed him with a haughty glare, "This is just an animal, my man, I will pay your bill, but do not try to teach me my business." "But Madame, I am trying to save your valuable property," said the Man, but she brushed him to silence as she read through the bill, clucking with displeasure at the items there. Then, opening her purse, she took out her check book and wrote something on a piece of paper before handing it to him. Rudely Mme. Diplomat turned and stalked off. "We have to live through this every day," whispered Madame Albertine to the Woman. They nodded in sympathy and drove slowly away.

Almost a week I had been away. Much must have happened during my absence. I spent the rest of the day going round from place to place renewing past associations, and reading all the news. For a time I rested snug and secure on a branch of my old friend the Apple Tree.

Supper was the usual scraps, of good quality, but still scraps. I thought how perfectly wonderful it would be to have something bought specially for me instead of always having "leavings." With the coming of dusk Gaston came in search of me, and having found me snatched me off the ground and hurried to the outhouse with me. Wrenching open the door, he flung me into the dark interior, slammed the door behind him, and departed. Being French myself, I am very greatly pained to admit that French humans are very hard indeed on animals.

Day ran into day and merged into weeks. Gradually I assumed a matronly figure and became slower in my movements. One night when I was almost at full term, I was roughly thrown into the outhouse by Pierre. As I landed on the hard concrete floor I felt a terrible pain, as if I were splitting. Painfully, in the darkness of that cold outhouse, my five babies were born. When I had recovered a little I shredded some paper and made a warm nest for them, then carried them one by one to it.

The next day no one came to see me. The day dragged on, but I was still busy feeding my babies. Night found me faint with hunger and absolutely parched, for there was neither food nor water in the outhouse. The following day brought no relief, no one came, and the hours dragged and dragged.

My thirst was almost unbearable and I wondered why I should have to suffer so. With nightfall the owls swooped and hooted about the mice they had caught. I, and my kittens lay together, and I wondered how I would live through the next day.

The day was well advanced when I heard footsteps. The door was opened, and there stood Madame Albertine looking pale and ill. She had got specially from her bed as she had had "visions" of me in trouble. As was her wont, she had brought food and water. One of my babies had died during the night, and Madame Albertine was almost too furious to speak. Her fury was so great at the manner in which I had been treated that she went and brought Mme. Diplomat and Monsieur le Duc. Mme. Diplomat's sorrow was at the loss of one kitten, and the loss of money which that meant. Monsieur le Duc managed a sickly smile and said, "Perhaps we can do something about it. Someone should speak to Pierre."

Gradually my children grew stronger; gradually they opened their eyes. People came to see them, money changed hands, and almost before they were weaned they were taken from me. I wandered inconsolable around the estate. My lamentations disturbed Mme. Diplomat and she ordered me to be shut up until I was quiet.

By now I was used to being shown off at social gatherings, and thought nothing of being taken from my work in the gardens in order to parade through the Salon. One day it was different. I was taken to a small room where Mme. Diplomat sat writing at a desk, and a strange man sat opposite her.

"Ah!" he exclaimed as I was brought into the room, "so this is the cat?" In silence he examined me, screwed up his face and played with one of his ears. "She is somewhat neglected. To drug her so that she can be carried as luggage aboard a plane will undermine her constitution." Mme. Diplomat scowled angrily at him; "I am not asking you for a lecture, Mister the Veterinarian," she said, "if you will not do as I ask many more will. Good Gracious!" she expostulated in fury, "What a fuss about a mere cat!" Mister the Veterinarian shrugged his shoulders helplessly, "Very well, Madame," he replied, "I will do as you wish, for I have my living to earn.

Call me an hour or so before you are due to board the plane." He rose to his feet, groped about for his case, and blundered out of the room. Mme. Diplomat opened the French windows and chased me into the garden.

There was an air of suppressed excitement about the house. Great cases were being dusted and cleaned, and Monsieur le Duc's new rank was being painted on them. A carpenter was called and told to make a wooden traveling box which would fit inside a case and capable of holding a cat. Madame Albertine fluttered around looking as if she hoped Mme. Diplomat would drop dead!

One morning, about a week later, Gaston came to the out-house for me and took me to the garage without giving me any breakfast. I told him I was hungry, but as usual he did not understand. Mme. Diplomat's maid, Yvette, was waiting in the Citroen. Gaston put me in a wicker basket with a strapped top, and I was lifted on to the back seat. We drove off at a very fast rate. "I don't know why she wants the cat drugged," said Yvette, "The Regulations say that a cat may be taken into the U.S.A. without any difficulties." "Aw," said Gaston, "That woman is crazy, I have given up trying to guess what makes HER tick!" They relapsed into silence and concentrated on driving faster and faster. The jouncing was terrible; my small weight was not enough to press down the seat springs, and I was becoming more and more bruised from hitting the sides and top of the basket.

I concentrated on keeping my legs outstretched, and sank my claws into the basket. Truly it was a grim battle to prevent myself from being knocked unconscious. I lost all count of time. Eventually we skidded to a screaming stop. Gaston grabbed my basket and rushed up some steps and into a house. The basket was plonked on to a table and the lid removed. Hands lifted me and set me down on the table.

Immediately I fell over, my legs would no longer support me, I had been tensed too long. Mister the Veterinarian looked at me in horror and compassion. "You could have killed this cat," he exclaimed angrily to Gaston, "I cannot give her an injection today!" Gaston's face flamed with anger. "Drug the * * * * * cat, the plane leaves today, you have been paid, haven't you?" Mister the Veterinarian picked up the telephone. "No use in you phoning," said Gaston, "The Family are at Le Bourget Airport, and I'm in a hurry." Sighing, Mister the Veterinarian picked up a big syringe and turned to me. I felt a sharp and painful stab deep within my muscles and the whole world turned blood red, then black. Faintly I heard a voice say, "There! That will keep her quiet for . . ." Then oblivion complete and utter descended upon me.

There was a dreadful roaring, I was cold and miserable, and breathing was a shocking effort. Not a gleam of light anywhere, I had never known such darkness. For a time I feared that I had gone blind. My head was splitting, never before had I felt so ill, so neglected, and so miserable.

Hour after hour the horrid roaring continued, I thought my brain would burst. There came strange pressures to my ears and things inside them went click and pop. The roaring changed, becoming fiercer, then there was a jarring clang and I was thrown violently to the top of my box. Another jar, and another and the roaring subsided. Now there came a strange rumbling, like the wheels of a fast car on a concrete highway. Strange jerks and rumbles, and then the roaring died. Other noises took over, the scraping of metal, muffled voices, and a chug-chug directly beneath me. With a shattering crash a great metal door opened beside me, and strange men came clattering in to the compartment where I was.

Rough hands grabbed cases and threw them on .to a moving belt which conveyed them out of sight. Then came my turn; I sailed through the air and landed with a bone jarring thud.

Beneath me something went 'rumble-rumble swish-swish.' A bang, and my journey stopped. I lay on my back and saw a dawn sky through some air holes. "Gee, dis heah's a cat!" said a strange voice. "Okay, Bud its not our worry," replied another man. Unceremoniously my case was grabbed and thrown on to some sort of vehicle. Other cases were piled around and on top, and the motor thing started off with a 'rumpf rumpf rumpf' noise. With the pain and the shock I lost consciousness.

I opened my eyes and found that I was gazing at a naked electric light bulb, gazing through wire netting. Weakly I struggled to my feet and tottered to a dish of water which I saw nearby. It was almost too much strain to drink, almost too much trouble to go on living, but having drunk I felt the better for it. "Well, well, Ma'am," said a wheezing voice, "So you is awake!" I looked and there was a little old black man opening a tin of food. "Yaas, Ma'am," he said, "You'n me we both got black faces, I guess I look after you good, eh?" He slipped the food in and I managed a weak purr to show that I appreciated his kindness. He stroked my head, "Gee, ain't dat sumpin!" he muttered to himself, "Jest wait till I tell Sadie, Man of man!"

To be able to eat again was wonderful. I could not manage much because I felt terrible, but I made an attempt so that the black man should not feel insulted. Then I had another peck and a drink, and after that I felt sleepy. There was a rug in the corner, so I curled up on it and went to sleep.

Eventually I found that I was in an hotel. Staff people kept coming down to the basement to see me. "Oh! Isn't she cute?" said the girl servants. "Wow! Just look at those eyes, man! Are they beautiful!" said the men. One visitor was very welcome, a French Chef. One of my admirers called through a telephone; "Hey, Françoise, come down here, we have a French Siamese Cat!" Minutes later a fat man waddled down the corridor, "You 'av ze chat francaise no?" he said to the men standing around. I purred louder and louder, it was quite a link with France to see him. He came over and peered short-sightedly and then burst into a torrent of Parisian French. I purred and yelled at him that I understood him perfectly. "Saay!" said a hushed voice, "Whadye- know? Old Francois and The Cat sure are hitting it off together on all cylinders."

The black man opened my cage door and I leaped straight into Francois' arms, he kissed me and I gave him some of my very best licks, and when I was put in the cage again he had tears in his eyes. "Ma'am," said my black attendant, "You sure ev made a hit. Guess you eat pretty good now." I liked my attendant, like me he had a black face. But pleasant things did not last for me. Two days later we moved to another city in the U.S.A. and I was kept in an underground cellar for almost the whole of my time. For the next several years life was the same day after day, month after month. I was used to produce kittens which were taken from me almost before I had them weaned.

At long last Monsieur le Duc was recalled to France. Once again I was drugged and knew no more until I awakened, sick and ill, at Le Bourget. Homecoming, to which I had looked with avid pleasure, was instead a sad affair. Madame Albertine was no longer there, she had died a few months before we returned. The Old Apple Tree had been cut down and much remodeling of the House had taken place.

For some months I wandered disconsolately around, bringing a few families into the world and seeing them taken from me before I was ready. My health began to fail and more and more kittens were born dead. My sight became uncertain, and I learned to "sense" my way round. Never did I forget that Tong Fa had been killed because he was old and blind!

When we had been back from America for almost two years, Mme. Diplomat wanted to go to Eire to see if it was a suitable place for her to live. She had the fixed idea that I had brought her luck (although she was no kinder to me for it!) and I had to go to Eire as well. Once again I was taken to a place where I was drugged, and for a time life ceased to exist for me. Much much later I woke up in a cloth lined box in a strange house. There was a constant drone of aircraft in the sky. The smell of burning peat tickled my nostrils and made me sneeze. "She is awake," said a broad Irish voice. What had happened? Where was I? Panic struck me but I was too weak to move. Only later, through hearing the talk of humans, and through being told by an Airport cat, did I get the story.

The plane had landed on the Irish Airport. Men had removed the luggage from the luggage compartment. "Hey, Paddy, there's an old dead cat in here!" said one of the men. Paddy, the foreman, moved to look. "Get the Inspector," he said. A man talked into his 'walkie-talkie' and soon an Inspector from the Animal Department came on the scene.

My box was opened and I was gently lifted out. "Get the Owner," said the Inspector. While waiting he examined me. Mme. Diplomat walked angrily over to the little group about me. Starting to bluster, and tell how important she was, she was soon cut short by the Inspector. "The cat is dead," he said, "killed by vicious cruelty and neglect. She is in kitten, and you have drugged her with a view to evading Quarantine. This is a serious offence."

Mme. Diplomat started to weep, saying that it would affect her husband's career if she were prosecuted for such an offence. The Inspector pulled at his bottom lip, then, on a sudden decision, said, "The animal is dead. Sign a waiver that we may dispose of the body and we will say no more about it this time. But I advise you NOT to keep cats again!"

Mme. Diplomat signed the proffered paper and walked off sniffing. "All right, Briari," said the Inspector, "Get rid of the body." He walked away and one of the men lifted me into the box again and carried me off. Very vaguely I heard the sound of earth being turned, the clink of metal on stone as perhaps a shovel scraped against an obstruction. Then I was lifted, and faintly heard, "Glory be! She is alive!" With that my consciousness faded again. The man, so I was told, looked about him surreptitiously, then, assured that he was unobserved, filled in the grave that he had dug for me, and hurried with me to a nearby house.

Nothing else was known to me until - "She is awake," said a broad Irish voice. Gentle hands stroked me, someone wet my lips with water. "Sean," said the Irish voice, "This cat is blind. I have been waving the light in front of her eyes and she does not see it." I was terrified, thinking they would kill me because of my age and sightlessness. "Blind?" said Sean, "Sure, 'tis a lovely creature she is. I'll go and see the Supervisor and get the rest of the day off. Sure and I'll be after taking her to my Mother, she will look after her. We can't keep her here." There was the sound of a door opening, and closing. Gentle hands held food just beneath my mouth and being famished, I ate. The pain inside me was terrible and I thought I would soon die.

My sight was gone completely. Later, when I lived with the Lama he spent much money to see what could be done, but it was then discovered that my optic nerves had been severed by the banging about that I had had.

The door opened and closed. "Well?" asked the woman. "I told the Supervisor I felt upset that one of God's creatures should be treated so." He said "Aw, sure, Sean, you always were a one to feel such things, yes, take time off." So here I am. "How is she doing?"

"Hmm, so so," answered his wife, "I wet her lips and she had a bite of fish. She will recover, but she has had a terrible time." The man fidgeted around, "Get me some food, Mary, and I will take the cat off to mother. I'll go out now and look to me tires." I sighed, MORE traveling, I wondered. The pain within me was a dull throbbing ache. Around me there was the clatter of dishes, and the sound of a fire being raked.

Presently the woman went to the door and called, "Tea, Sean, the kettle is on the boil". Sean came in and I heard him wash his hands before settling down to his meal.

"We have got to keep this quiet," said Sean, "or we shall have the Garda after us. If we can get her well, her kittens will bring us money. These creatures are valuable, you know." His wife poured another cup of tea before answering.

"Your mother knows all about cats, she will bring this one round if anyone will. Get yourself gone before the others come off work." "Aye, that I will," said Sean as he pushed back his chair noisily and rose to his feet. They came over to me and I felt my box being lifted. "You can't put the box on the carrier, Sean," said the woman, "keep it under your arm, I will fix a sling so that you can take the weight across your shoulders, not that SHE has much weight, poor little soul!"

Sean, with a strap across his shoulders and around my box, turned and left the house. The cool Irish air wafted wonder- fully into my box, carrying an invigorating tang of the sea.

It made me feel much better -- if only the dreadful pain would go away! A ride on a bicycle was an absolutely new experience to me. A gentle breeze came through the air-holes and there was a slight swaying which was not unpleasing, it reminded me of lying on the high branches of a tree which was swaying in the wind. A most curious creaking noise puzzled me for some time. At first I thought that my box was falling apart, then by concentrating carefully I decided that the seat-thing upon which Sean sat needed oil. Soon we came to rising ground. Sean's breath began to rasp in his throat, the pedals moved slower and slower, eventually slowing to a stop. "Ah, Begob!" he exclaimed, "tis a heavy box you have!" Resting my box on the saddle -- yes, it DID squeak! -- he trudged on up the hill, slowly pushing the bicycle. Stopping, he unlatched a gate, and pushed the bicycle through, there was the scrape of wood against metal, and the gate slammed shut behind us. "What am I going in to now?" I wondered. The pleasant smell of flowers came to my nostrils; I sniffed appreciatively.

"And what have ye brought me, my son?" asked an elderly voice. "I've brought Herself to you, Mother," replied Sean proudly. Resting the machine against a wall, he lifted my box, carefully wiped his feet and entered a building. With a sigh of relief he sat down and told his mother the whole story, so far as he knew it, about me. Fumbling with the box lid he threw it back. For a moment there was silence. Then, "Ah! 'tis a wonderful creature she must have been in her heyday. Look at her now, with her coat rough with neglect. Look at her ribs showing. Ah! 'tis a cruel shame to treat creatures so!"

At last I was lifted out and set upon the floor. It is disconcerting to suddenly lose one's sight. First, as I took my staggering steps, I bumped into things. Sean muttered, "Mother, d'ye think we should -- YOU know!" "No, my son, no, these are very intelligent cats, VERY intelligent cats indeed. You will remember I told you I had seen them in England. No no, give her time, she will manage." Sean turned to his mother, "Mother, I am going to take the box back and turn it in to the Supervisor in the morning, you know." The old woman bustled about, bringing food and water and -- most necessary, leading me to a box of earth! Eventually Sean departed with a promise to come in a few days time. The old woman carefully locked the door and threw another lump of peat on the fire, mumbling to herself all the time in what I took to be the Irish language. To cats, of course, language does not matter much because we converse and listen by telepathy. Humans THINK in their own language and it is sometimes a little confusing for a French Siamese cat to sort out thought-pictures framed in some other language.

Soon we lay down to sleep, I in a box beside the fire, and the old woman on a couch at the far side of the room. I was utterly exhausted, yet the pain gnawing within me prevented sleep. Eventually tiredness overcame the pain, and I drifted off. My dreams were terror-wracked. What had I come to?

I wondered in my dream state, why had I to suffer so? I feared for my kittens-to-come. Feared that they would die at birth, feared that they would not, for what future had they? Could I, in my weakened state, feed them?

Morning found the old woman stirring. The couch springs creaked as she rose and came over to poke the fire. Kneeling beside me, she stroked my head and said, "Tis meself that will be going to Mass, then we will have a bite to eat." She rose to her feet and soon left the room. I heard her footsteps fading away down the path. There was the 'click' of the garden gate, then silence. I turned over and slept again.

By the end of the day my strength had returned somewhat. I was able to move around slowly. First I bumped into almost everything, but I soon learned that furniture was not often moved. In time I became quite adept at finding my way round without getting too many bruises. Our vibrissae ("cats' whiskers") act like radar and we can find our way about in the darkest of dark nights, when there is no glimmer of light by which to see. Now my vibrissae had to work overtime!

A few days later the old woman said to her son, who had called to see her, "Sean, clean out the woodshed, I am going to keep her in there. What with her being blind, and me not seeing well either, I am afraid I may kick her and hurt the kittens -- and they are worth many pounds to us!" Sean walked out and soon I heard a commotion from the wood- shed as he moved things round and stacked up piles of peat.

He came in and said, "It is all ready, Mother, I have put piles of newspapers on the floor and stopped up the window." So -- once again my bed was of newspapers. Irish ones this time.

"Well," I thought, "Apple Tree years ago said deliverance would come at my blackest hour. It should be almost time!" The woodshed was of tarred planks with a rickety door. The floor was of beaten earth, and along the walls was stored a remarkable collection of household effects, peat slabs and empty boxes. For some peculiar reason the old woman used a truly immense padlock with which to keep the door closed. Whenever she .came to see me she stood and muttered and fiddled endlessly with keys until she found the correct one. With the door open at last, she would stumble in, feeling her way into the gloomy interior. Sean wanted to repair the window so there would be some light -- no rays entered this dark hole -- but as the old woman said, "Glass costs money, my son, glass costs money. Wait until we have the kittens to sell!"

The days crawled on. I had food and water, but I was constantly in pain. Food was scarce, enough to keep me alive, but not enough to build up my strength. I lived to give birth to my kittens, and staying alive was a struggle. Blind, ill, and always hungry, I maintained a tenuous hold of life and faith in those "better days to come!"

A few weeks after I arrived in Ireland I knew that soon m kittens would be born. Movement became difficult, and the pain increased. No longer could I stretch at full length, or curl into a circle. Something had happened inside me and I could rest only sitting up, with my chest resting on some- thing hard in order to keep weight off my lower parts.

Two or three nights later, at about midnight, really terrible pain assailed me. I screamed in agony. Slowly, with immense effort, my kittens came into the world. Three of the five were dead. For hours I lay gasping, my whole body as if aflame. This, I thought, was the end of my life, but no, it was not to be. I lived on.

The old woman came into the shed in the morning and said terrible things when she found three dead kittens. She said such terrible things that she afterwards said a prayer for forgiveness! I thought that now, with two very little kittens to nurse, I would be able to go in the house where there was warmth and something more than newspapers to lie upon.

But the old woman appeared to hate me for having only two live kittens. "Sean," she said one evening to her son, "this cat won't live more than two or three weeks. See if you can spread it around that I have two Siamese kittens for sale."

Daily I grew weaker; I longed for death but feared for my kittens. One day, when they were almost weaned, a car drew up at the gate. From my shed I could hear all. I heard the gate click open and two people walked up the little path. A knock at the cottage door. Seconds later it opened. A woman's voice said, "I understand you have a Siamese kitten for sale." "Ah, now, and will ye come in?" replied the old woman. For a time there was silence, then the old woman came shambling out and grabbed one of my children.

Minutes later she came back, muttering bad-temperedly, "An' what would he want to be seeing you for?" She snatched me up so violently that I screamed with pain. With a show of great affection she carried me into the house. Gentle voices spoke my name, and very lightly touched me. The Man said, "We want to take the Mother as well. She will not live unless she is treated." "Ah!" said the old woman, "'tis a very healthy and good cat she is!" From the old woman's mind I read her thoughts : "Yes," she thought, "I have read all about you, you can pay plenty." She made a great fuss, saying how much she loved me and how valuable I was.

How she did not want to sell me. I turned in the Man's direction and said, "I'm dying, just ignore me and look after my two children." The Man turned to the old woman and said, "Did you say you had two kittens?" She admitted she had, so the Man said, firmly, We will take all three cats or none." The old woman named a price which staggered me, but the Man just said, "All right, get them ready, we will take them now." The old woman left the room in a hurry in order to conceal her delight and so that she could count the money again. Soon my two boys were placed in a very special basket which the Man and the Woman had brought. The Woman sat in the back of the car, with me on her lap, and the big basket was placed on the front seat beside the Man.

Slowly, carefully, we drove off. "We shall have to get the Vet to see Fifi right away, Rab," said the Man. "She is very sick, I'll phone as soon as we get home, he'll come today.

Shall we let the kittens go together?" "Yes," said the Man, "then they will not be lonely." We drove on so carefully that I felt no pain. The words of the Apple Tree came back to me, "You will know happiness, Fifi." Was this IT? I wondered.

We rolled along the road for many miles, then carefully turned a sharp corner and started up a steep hill. "Well, we are home, cats," said the Man. Stopping the engine, he got out and carried away the basket containing my kittens. The Woman carefully got out, without jarring me, and carried me up three or four steps into a house. What a difference!

Here I felt at once that I was wanted and welcome, I decided that the Tree was right. But I felt so dreadfully weak. The Woman went to a telephone and I heard her speaking to the Vet that had been mentioned. With a word of thanks she rang off. "He is coming right away," she said.

I do not propose to write of my operation, nor of the long struggle back to life. It will suffice to say that I had a most difficult operation to remove an immense uterine tumor. I had a hysterectomy and so was free from the hardship of having babies any more. The Man and the Woman stayed up with me for night after night, for the operation was so severe that it was thought I would not recover. I knew differently, because now I was Home -- and wanted.

Chapter Four

My operation was behind me, all I had to do now was to recover. Previously I had been too ill to bother WHO lived in the house or what it was like. Mister the Irish Vet had said, "You must take her home and give her love, she is starved for it, and she will not live if we keep her here." So -- Home I was taken. For the first two days and nights I was kept very quiet indeed, with the Man and the Woman nursing me all the time and persuading me to taste the choicest food. I did not take it too easily, because I WANTED to be persuaded, I WANTED to know that they thought enough of me to take the time necessary to persuade me!

One morning of the third day after Mister the Irish Vet had been, the Man said, "I'm going to bring in the Lady Ku'ei, Feef." He went out and soon returned, murmuring affectionately to someone. As they drew near he said, "Feef, this is the Lady Ku'ei. Ku, this is Mrs. Fifi Greywhiskers." Immediately I heard the most beautiful Young Lady Siamese Cat voice it has been my pleasure to hear. The range! The power! I was enthralled and wished that my poor dear Mother could have heard such a voice. The Lady Ku'ei sat on the bed with the Man sitting between us. "I am the Lady Ku'ei," she said, "But as we are going to live together you may call me MISS Ku'ei. You are blind, so when you are able to walk I will take you around and point out obstacles, 'the facilities,' where you eat, etcetera. And in connection with that," she remarked in a self satisfied tone, "here we do NOT eat scraps, nor do we rake out the garbage (when anyone is looking), our food is purchased specially for us and is of the best quality. Now pay great attention, for I am going to brief you on the household, and I shall not say it twice."

"Yes, Miss Ku," I replied humbly, "I give you my whole attention." I eased myself slightly in order to release the pressure on my stitches.

"This is Howth, County Dublin," commenced Miss Ku, "We live in a house perched right on top of a cliff. The sea is a hundred and twenty feet below us -- straight down, so don't fall over or people will be annoyed if you should hit a fish. You must maintain your dignity with visitors -- remember you are a P.S.C. -- but you may romp freely with The Family."

"Please Miss Ku," I interjected, "What is a P.S.C.?"

"Well! Well! You ARE a stupid Old Woman Cat," replied Miss Ku, "ANYONE would know that P.S.C. indicates that you are a Pedigree Siamese Cat -- although you are not showing the intelligence expected of one. But don't interrupt, I'm giving you the essential information." "I'm sorry, Miss Ku, I won't interrupt you again," I answered.

Miss Ku thoughtfully scratched her ear with her foot and continued, "The 'Man' as you call him is the Lama T. Lobsang Rampa of Tibet. He understands Siamese Cats as well as you and I do, so you cannot keep your thoughts from him. He is big, bearded and bald and he is nearly dead in his heart with a coronary or two. He has been very ill indeed and we all thought we would lose him." I nodded gravely, knowing what it was like to be ill. Miss Ku continued, "If you have troubles, tell him and he will help you straighten out. If you want any particular food, tell him, he will pass on the news to Ma."

"Ma?" I queried, "Is your Mother with you?"

"Don't be so ridiculous!" replied Miss Ku with some asperity, "Ma is Rab, the Woman, you know, the one who does our shopping, cleans our tins, makes our beds, cooks for us, and lets us sleep on her bed. I'm her cat, you know, you are the Lama's cat," said Miss Ku smugly. "You will sleep in this room, beside him. Oh, of course, you cannot see Ma. She is a bit short, nice eyes and nice ankles and a comfortable plumpness everywhere else. No bones will stick into you when you sit on HER lap!"

We paused for a moment, Miss Ku to recover her breath, and I to absorb the information passed to me so suddenly. Miss Ku idly played with the end of her tail and continued, "We have a Young English Lady living with us as one of the family. She is very tall, very thin, and has hair the color of a marmalade Tom I once saw. Quite kind, though, and she will give you your dues although she DOES like big smelly dogs and screaming children."

"Now, Ku'ei," said the Lama, "Feef has to rest, you can tell her some more later."

He picked up Miss Ku and carried her out of the room. For a time I lay on his bed, purring with contentment. No more scraps -- I'd always thought I would like to have something bought specially for me. To be wanted, that had been my ambition throughout the long lean years. Now I WAS wanted, very much so. I smiled contentedly and dropped off to sleep. As my operation wounds healed, and the stitches were removed, I was able to move about more and more. Very cautiously at first, because of my sightlessness, but with more assurance when I found that nothing was moved unless I was first taken to it and shown its position in relation to other things. Miss Ku'ei went about with me, telling me where every thing was, and people who came were cautioned that I was blind.

"What!" they would reply, "Blind? But she has such big beautiful blue eyes, how can she be blind?"

At last I was considered well enough to be taken into the garden. The air was beautiful, with the smell of the sea and the plants. For many days I would not let anyone get between me and the door, I was constantly afraid that I should be shut out.

Miss Ku would chide me, "Don't be such an old fool, Feef, we are PEOPLE here, no one will shut you out --ever."

We would lie in the warm grass and Miss Ku would describe the scene for me. Below us the tumbling waves, reaching up towards us with fingers of white spume. Water in the cave beneath the house grumbled and roared and, on stormy days, seemed to shake the whole cliff. To the left was the sea wall, with the lighthouse at the end. A mile or so across the water Ireland's Eye stood sheltering the little harbor from the worst buffets of the turbulent Irish Sea. To the right the Devil's Tooth projected a few yards from the main mass of land, protecting the Mens' Bathing Place from the heavier waves. Miss Ku loved to watch the men bathing, perhaps I should also if I had had my sight.

Behind the house reared the peak of the Hill of Howth, from the top of which, on a clear day, could often be seen the mountains of Wales, on the mainland, and the Mountains of Mourne in Northern Ireland. These were happy days, as we lazed in the sunlight and Miss Ku told me of Our Family.

Gradually I lost my fears that I would be shut out. No longer did I have to be sent to a great rough Tom. Now I was wanted for myself alone, and

-- as Miss Ku herself said -- I expanded under the influence like a flower taken into the sunlight after being in the darkness of a lonely cellar. We loved those days, the Lama would put me on the lowest branches of a small tree and hold me so that I could not fall, and I would dream that here at last I had entered Heaven. The gulls bothered me at first, as they swooped over they would scream and say "Look at that cat down there, dive on her, drive her over the cliff and then we will eat her." Miss Ku would growl our famous Siamese War Cry and would unsheath her claws ready for any attack. Faintly on the air would come a "thug-thug, thug-thug" and all the birds overhead would wheel madly and rush off. For long this puzzled me greatly, I could not always be asking questions, then I found the answer. The fishing boats were coming in and the birds were after the fish offal being washed from the decks.

I was lazing in the warm shade of a Veronica bush one sunny afternoon when Miss Ku called, "Get yourself ready, Feef, we are going for a drive." A DRIVE ? In a CAR? I almost fainted with horror and astonishment. A CAR and Miss Ku'ei was PLEASED! "But Miss Ku," I expostulated, "I simply COULDN'T go in a car. What if they left me somewhere!"

"FEEF!" called the Lama, "Come on, we are all going for a ride." I was so faint with fright that I had to be picked up and carried to the car. Not so Miss Ku, she sang with joy; rushed into the car and yelled, "I bag the front seat!" "Is the Lama going to drive, Miss Ku?" I asked timidly. "Of course he is, and don't say 'the Lama' all the time, say 'Guv' the same as I do."

Sure enough the Lama, sorry -- the Guv -- got into the car and sat on a front seat beside Miss Ku. Ma got in the car and sat at the back, taking me on her lap. The Young English Lady (I could not say her name yet) sat beside Ma. "Sure you have locked the doors?" asked the Guv. "Of course, don't we always?" replied Ma.

"Come on, come on, what are we wasting time for?" shrieked Miss Ku. The Guv did whatever one has to do to make the car start and we moved off. I was amazed at the smoothness of our progress. This was far different from being thrown violently from side to side as had been my experience in France and America. We moved down a steep hill and turned a very sharp corner. Rolling along for perhaps -- what was it here? Miles? Kilometers? -- three or four minutes we turned sharp right, went for another minute or so and stopped. The engine was turned off. The smell of the sea was strong. Light spray, blown on the breeze, tickled my nostrils. Sounds of many men, sounds of thug- thug engines.

A strong smell of fish and of fish that had been too long in the sunlight. Smell of smoke and of tarred rope.

"Ah! Lovely fish!" breathed the Young English Lady, "Shall I go in and get some?" So off she went to see an old friend who would sell us fish straight from the sea. CLANG! went the luggage-thing at the back as the wrapped fish were dropped in. BANG! went the door as the Young English Lady got in the car and slammed the door shut. "Miss Ku!"

I whispered "What is this place?" "This? This is the harbor where all the fishing boats come to bring our supper. Big storage sheds by the side of us, water at the other side. Ships tied up with bits of rope so they can't go off until everyone is ready. That smoke? Oh, they stick fish in some smoke, they don't go bad so quickly that way -- or you can't smell it so quickly because of the smoke." She jumped up on the back of the Guv's seat and yelled, "WHAT ARE WE WAITING FOR? Let us go to Partmarnock." "Oh Ku, you are an impatient wretch!" said the Guv, starting the car thing again and moving it off.

"Miss Ku!" I said in, I'm afraid, rather worried tones, "This Young English Lady, I cannot say her name, and the way I pronounce it it is a curse on a too-eager Tom. What shall I do?" Miss Ku sat and thought for a while and then said, "Well, I don't know, I'm sure." Suddenly she perked up and said, "Hey! I know! She has on a green frock, she is very tall and thin and the hair on top is sort of yellow: Hey, Feef, call her BUTTERCUP -- she won't know!" "Thank you, Miss Ku," I replied, "I will refer to her as Miss Buttercup." "Miss nothing," retorted Miss Ku, "We should miss Buttercup, but she is Missus, like you, she has had kittens too. No, Feef, you are not in French polite society now. You are HOME, so say 'Guv', 'Ma', and 'Buttercup.' I am MISS Ku."

The car rolled on, gently, smoothly. Almost before I knew what was happening we had reached 'there' and stopped. The doors of the car were opened and I was lifted out. "Ah! This is the LIFE!" yelled Miss Ku. Gentle hands took mine and shuffled them through the sand. "Look Feef, sand," said the Guv. The roar and swish of the waves against the rocks soothed me, the sun was warm on my back. Miss Ku was scampering madly up and down the sand, yelling her joy.

The Family (MY Family) sat quietly by. I sat at their feet and toyed with a pebble. I was too old and had not ye healed enough to run with wild whoops like Miss Ku. With the comfort and warm sunlight I fell asleep.

Clouds were over the sun, there was a faint drizzle of rain. "Strange!" I thought, "How can I be HERE?" Then it came to me, I was Astral Traveling. Light as a cloud I drifted along over coastal roads, moving inland. The great Airport at Le Bourget, inland, inland. A long row of poplar trees still standing sentinel along the straight white road. The spire of the church, half shrouded with mist and the trees in the graveyard weeping in the rain for those who lay beneath.

I drifted, wraithlike myself, drifted and came lower. Suddenly I saw, for one is not blind in the Astral, "Sacred to the Memory of. . ."For a moment I was at a loss, then com- prehension hit me. "MADAME ALBERTINE!" I shouted. "Buried here!" A sob escaped me. THEN she had been the only one to love me. Now she was gone and I had come into happiness and love. But then, I thought, she had gone from this wicked world and entered into love and happiness herself. With a sigh and a last look I again rose and drifted on.

Beneath me the Lodgekeeper was sweeping a courtyard at the back of his Lodge. A dog, chained to the wall, growled and whined uneasily at my passing. The House loomed before me, stately, cold, unfriendly, as if forbidding one to enter. Mme. Diplomat came out on to the terrace. Instinctively I turned to run, but of course she did not see me hovering at shoulder-height. She looked thin and haggard. Great lines of discontent marred her features. The ends of her mouth turned sharply down, and with thin lips and pinched nostrils she looked bitter indeed.

I moved on, moved toward the Old Apple Tree, and halted in shocked horror. The Tree was gone, felled, and even the stump had been extracted: Silently, sorrowing, I hovered around. Moved by some inexplicable impulse I drifted towards the old outhouse which had been my only home. My heart almost stopped; the remains of my friend the Apple Tree were piled against one wall as firewood. A movement at the door, and there was Pierre, axe in hand upraised. I screamed and faded from that place .

"There! There! Feef," said the Guv as he lifted me to his shoulder and walked around with me. "You have had a nightmare -- in the sunlight, too. I'm surprised at you, Feef!" I shuddered, and felt sudden gratitude.

Turning my head I licked his ear. He carried me down to the waters edge and stood there, with me on his shoulder. "I know what you feel, Feef," he said, "I've been through hardships as well, you know." Stroking my back, he turned and walked over to the others. "Shall we get back?" he asked, "Old Granny Greywhiskers is getting tired." I purred and purred and PURRED. It was just wonderful having someone who thought of me, who could TALK to me. We all got in the car and we started back on the journey home.

I suppose I am a cranky old woman cat, or something, but I have a few phobias. Even now I do not like motor cars. Being blind has something to do with it, but I still have a fear that I am going to be left somewhere. Miss Ku'ei is poised, an experienced society lady whom nothing ruffles. At all times she is completely master (or mistress?) of the situation. I -- well, as I say, I am sometimes a little eccentric. That makes it all the more wonderful that they love me so. It is fortunate that they do, because now I cannot BEAR to be alone. For years I was starved of affection and now I want all there is to spare!

Over the Hill of Howth we drove, along where the tram tracks meandered by the side of the road. To the highest point and beyond. Down to the village, turn right before reaching the big Church, past Mr. and Mrs. O'Grady's house, another left and we are home. Dear old Mr. Loftus, "our" policeman, was looking over the wall. Never did we pass him without speaking, for the Guv said Mr. Loftus was one of the best men in Ireland or anywhere else!

I was tired, glad to get home. All I wanted was some food, something to drink, and then sleep on the Guv's bed, with the sound of the waves lulling me, reminding me of the time my Mother sang me to sleep. The last I heard before dropping off was Miss Ku, "Hi! I want to go down to the garage with you and put away the car." The soft shutting of a door, and all was quiet. It was wonderful sleeping, knowing that no one was coming to chase me or carry me off to a dark wood- shed. Knowing that I was respected as if I were a human, had the same rights as everyone else in the house. With a sigh of contentment, I curled up and snored a little louder.

"FEEF! Granny Greywhiskers! Get off that bed, the Guv wants to get in." "Ku'ei, don't be such a bully, CERTAINLY Fifi can stay on the bed. Now STOP it!" The Guv sounded cross. I raised my head so that I could hear better, then guessed where the floor was and jumped off. Gentle but firm hands caught me and lifted me back. "Now Feef! You are as bad as Ku'ei. Stay on the bed and keep me company." I stayed.

The Lama (sorry, Guv!) was a very sick man. Some time before he had had T.B. (one of my children had died from that, years ago), and although he had been cured it had left his lungs permanently impaired. He had had coronary thrombosis three times and he had other troubles as well. Like me, he had to rest a lot. Sometimes in the night he would walk up and down the room in pain; I would walk beside him, trying to console him. Those long hours of the night were the worst, when we were alone. I slept much through the daylight hours so that I could be with him in the nights.

Ma slept in a room at the other end of the house, and Miss Ku looked after her. Buttercup slept in a room downstairs where she could look out far over the Irish Sea and, in the mornings, see the Liverpool Boat steam toward the Port of Dun Laoghaire.

The Guv and I slept in a room overlooking Balscadden Bay, overlooking the Harbor and the Irish Sea. He would lie for hours on his bed watching the ever-changing scene with his powerful Japanese binoculars. Our very great friend Brud Campbell, had taken out the poor glass originally in place, and inserted instead the finest plate-glass so that there was no distortion of the view. As we sat together, him scanning the view, he would tell me all he saw, putting it into telepathic thought-pictures so that I could see as clearly as he. Ireland's Eye, he would tell me of the brave monks who years ago had tried to make a little church there, but had at last been defeated by the storms.

Miss Ku told me of Ireland's Eye as well. She had been brave enough to go with the Guv in a little boat all the way across the water and play in the sand on the Island. She told me of Pirate Cats who lived on the Island and frightened the birds and the rabbits. The Guv did not tell me of the Pirate Cats (perhaps he did not think cats would sink so low), but he did tell me of human smugglers, and he could even name them. Quite a lot of smuggling was done in the district, and the Guv knew almost everyone connected with it, he had taken many photographs with a telephoto camera.

Ma did photography, too, and wherever she went she carried a camera in her handbag. But Ma's chief concern was to look after us all and try to keep the Guv going for a few more years.

She was busy all the time. Miss Ku, of course, supervised everything and saw that no one slacked and that she got all the car rides that she wanted.

Buttercup was very busy as well. She helped look after the house and the Guv and she took long walks so that she could get ideas for drawing and painting. She is a very clever artist, Miss Ku and the Guv tell me. That is why I asked her to illustrate this little book of mine and Miss Ku says that she is doing it better than anyone else could. I wish I could see them, but no one can give me sight.

We loved to get the Guv in bed before he had a heart attack, and then have Mr. Loftus come and talk to him. Mr. Loftus was a great big man, tall and broad, and ALL of us admired him immensely. Miss Ku, who has given me per- mission to say that she is a bit of a flirt, loved him. Mrs. O'Grady was another welcome visitor, one who would drop in at any time. One who was accepted as "one of the family."

Brud Campbell did not call nearly as often as we would have liked, he was a busy man -- busy because he was such a good workman -- and his visits were all too few. One day we were discussing travel, and air travel in particular. Miss Ku said, "Oh, but when we came from England (with cries of joy!) the airline would not have CATS in the same compartment as humans. The Guv said: 'All right, then if they don't want my cat they do not want me, we will charter a plane and take all our things as well.' " Miss Ku paused for dramatic effect, and continued, "So we came by chartered plane and they had a bottle of oxygen for the Guv and he got cross at Dublin Airport because they wanted to put him in a wheel-chair as an invalid!" It gave me a warm feeling inside to know that The Family thought as much of Miss Ku -- and me! -- as they did of any human. Then we smiled as the Guv chuckled at us and told us that we were a gossiping pair of old woman cats!

"Miss Ku," I said one morning, "Mrs. O'Grady comes here a lot, but why does not MR. come here?" "Oh dear dear!" replied Miss Ku, "He has to work, he looks after the electricity of Ireland and if he didn't pour it in the wires how would we cook?" "But Miss Ku, we use gas in a metal thing and men bring the metal things here once every three weeks."

Miss Ku sighed in exasperation; "Feef," she said, after taking a deep breath to calm herself like the Guv had shown us. "Feef, people SEE, and if they are to see they use electricity. Right? You don't see, so you don't know. We have glass bottles tied to poles and hanging from the ceilings.

When people tip electricity into them from the wires we get a light. WE USE ELECTRICITY, Feef!" She turned away with a muttered, "Cats make me sick, always asking fool questions." We used electricity all right, the Guv and Ma took a lot of color photographs and showed them on a screen with a special lamp. I loved to sit with my back to the lamp, facing the screen, because the rays from the lamp were beautifully warm.

We did not have a telephone at Howth, someone told me that the Irish telephone people had no lines to spare. I could not understand why they did not put up more, like other countries did, but it did not matter to me. We used Mrs. O'Grady's phone, which was offered so gladly. Ma was VERY fond of "Ve O'G" as we called her. The Guv liked her as well, but he saw more of Mr. Loftus. From the big picture window overlooking the bay Mr. Loftus could be seen coming round the corner at the bottom of the steep hill, then trudging up Balscadden Road and right away to the end where all the picnickers went. When he went off duty he would often call in to see us -- and he was always a welcome visitor. The Guv would be in bed, and Mr. Loftus would sit facing him and the window.

We listened to the world, too! The Guv had a very powerful short-wave radio set which would bring in programs from China,

Japan, India -- and the Irish Police and Fire Stations! I preferred music from Siam, or Thailand, or whatever they now call the country of my ancestors. To the music of Siam I would sit and sway and gently keep time with my head. I would see in my mind's eye the temples, the fields and the trees. I would look back at the whole history of my ancestors. Some of us went to Tibet (where the Guv came from) and there we guarded the Temples and the lamaseries.

Like the proctors of Tibet, we too were trained to discourage thieves, and safeguard the jewels and the religious objects. In Tibet we were almost black because of the intense cold. It is perhaps not generally known that my race alter in color according to the temperature. In a cold, frozen country we grow very, very dark. In the tropical countries we are almost white. Our kittens are born pure white, and soon after the characteristic 'markings' appear. Just as humans have different colors, such as white, yellow, brown and black, so have we. I am a seal-pointed cat, while Miss Ku'ei is a chocolate-pointed cat. Her Father was, indeed, the Champion, Chocolate Soldier. Miss Ku had a very wonderful pedigree. My papers, of course, had been lost. Miss Ku and I were discussing it one day. "I wish I could show you my papers, Miss Ku," I said, "It grieves me to think they have been left in France. I feel, well, kind of NAKED without them." "There! There! Feef," soothed Miss Ku, "Think nothing of it. I will have a word with the Guv and ask him to destroy mine, then BOTH of us will be paperless." Before I could expostulate she had wheeled round and stalked out of the room. I heard her going down the stairs to where the Guv was doing something with a long brass tube which had glass at both ends. It seemed that he put the thing to one eye so that he could see better farther. Shortly after, the Guv and Miss Ku came up, still arguing. "Oh well," he said, "If that is the way you want it -- you always were a crazy cat!" He went to a drawer and I heard the rustling of papers and then the rasping of a match being struck. The smell of burning paper reached me and then the clatter of fire irons as the ashes were stirred into nothingness. Miss Ku came over and gave me a push. "Okay," she said with a smile, "Now stop your stupid worry. The Guv and Ma do not care a hang for these papers, or pedigrees, WE are THEIR children."

My nose wrinkled, and I sneezed. There was a beautiful smell in the air, something I had never smelled before.

"Feef! Where are you, Feef?" Ma was calling me. I told her that I was coming as I jumped off the bed. Following my nose -- being led by that wonderful smell -- I went down the stairs, "Lobster, Feef," said Ma. "Try it!"

Our kitchen had a stone floor and the Guv once told Miss Ku and me that there was a story to the effect that a passage under the flagstones connected the kitchen with the cave below. It made me nervous in case some pirate or smuggler should push up the stone from beneath and I should fall through. But Ma had called, and called for a new sort of food. Being a French Siamese Cat I had a natural interest in food. Ma tweaked my ears with affection and led me to the dish of lobster. Miss Ku was already at hers. "Get crackin' Feef," she said, "You are poking around like a real old Irish Biddy!" Of course I was never upset by what Miss Ku said she had a heart as good as the purest shrimp meat, and she had taken me, a dying, destitute stranger, into her home with gladness. For all her sternness, for all her autocratic manner, she was a person whom to know was to love.

The lobster was delicious! "From Ireland's Eye, Feef," said Miss Ku, "The Guv thought we would like it for a treat." "Oh!" I replied, "Doesn't he eat it?" "Never! Thinks it is horrible muck. Still, if you and I like it he will buy it for us. Remember those shrimps, Feef?" I did indeed! When the Guv and Ma first brought me to the house I was hungry, but almost too ill to eat. "Give her a tin of shrimps," said the Guv, "She is weak with hunger." The tin was opened, but I really could not be bothered. The Guv took a shrimp and wiped it across my lips. I thought I had never tasted any- thing more heavenly. Almost before I knew it, I had cleared the whole tin. It made me really ashamed of myself and I grow hot even now whenever I think of it. If Miss Ku wants to make me blush she says, "Remember those shrimps, Feef?"

"Feef!" said Miss Ku, "The Guv is going to take us for a ride. We are going past the cottage where you lived. Now don't throw a fit; we are going PAST." Miss Ku went out to walk down to the garage with the Guv to get the car, a good Humber Hawk. I stayed with Ma, helping her get ready, then went downstairs to make sure that Buttercup had locked the garden gate at the side. We got in the car and drove down the hill, under the tram bridge and on to Sutton (where another old friend, Dr. Chapman, lived). On we went, covering many miles and eventually reaching Dublin. Miss Ku helped the Guv drive, telling him when to go fast, what cars were about, and which turnings to take. I learned a lot from her. I learned about Dublin. In between directing the Guv -- "Stop! Stop! Mind this corner, quick! Don't let that car pass" she described the sights for me. "Now here is Westland Row Station, Feef, where the trains go from. We turn right here, Guv. Yes Feef, we are now in Nassau Street.

Slow up, Guv, I'm telling Feef about this. We used to live here, Feef, opposite Trinity College grounds. Guv you are going so fast I can't tell Feef This is St. Stephen's Green, I've been in there. Ducks quack in that place. Mind, Guv, there is a Garda on the corner. We get our radios down that street, Feef." On we went through the streets of Dublin, Miss Ku giving a running commentary. Then, with streets and houses behind us, the Guv pressed down something with a foot and the car ran faster as more food went into it.

Along the mountain roads we went, along by the side of what Miss Ku called "a reservoir" which seemed to be a drinking bowl for Dublin. We came to the cottage. The car stopped. The Guv glanced in my direction and seeing how I was affected, speeded up. I breathed with relief, half fearing, in spite of all, that I was going to be returned as a useless old blind cat. To show my happiness I purred and licked Ma's hand. "Great Tomcats! Feef," said Miss Ku, "We thought you were going to throw a fit and pass away in the odor of sanctity! Brace up, Old Girl, YOU ARE A MEMBER OF THE FAMILY!"

We played among the heather for a time. Miss Ku shouting about how many rabbits she was going to catch. Then she saw what the Guv said was a sheep, and fell abruptly silent. I could not see the creature, but I did detect a strange muttony smell and the odor of old wool. Soon we got in the car and went speeding off again on the way home. As we passed the Bailey Lighthouse, on Howth Head, the fog horn was bellowing like a cow about to give birth. A tram rumbled by, its wheels going 'clanketyclank, clankety- clank' on the iron rails. "Stop at the Post Office," said Ma "There should be some parcels there."

"Feef," said Miss Ku as we waited for Ma, "Feef, a man told the Guv your two kittens are doing fine. They are growing well and have black faces and tails now." I sighed with content. Life was good to me: My children were happy, and together. They were the last kittens I would ever have, and I was proud of them, proud that they had been accepted, and that they were happy.

Chapter Five

"Ah! Good Marnin' to ye," said Pat the Postman when Ma and I answered the door to his ring. "Tis a wunnerful lot of letters I have for Himself this marnin' -- nigh broke me back it did, carrying it up th' hill!" Pat the Postman was an old friend of ours. Many is the time the Guv picked him up in the car and drove him on his rounds when his legs were giving out with the walking. Pat knew everything and everybody in the district, and we picked up much local color from him. I used to smell his trouser turn-ups so that I could read of his walk across the Head, or through the heather banks. I used to know, too, when Pat had had "a little drop" to keep him warm on his evening round.

Ma carried in the letters and I got on the Guv's bed so that I could help him read them. There WERE a lot this morning, letters from Japan, from India, from friends in Germany.

A letter from -- Dublin. There was the sound of an envelope being slit, and paper dragged out. "Hmm!" said the Guv, "The Irish Tax officials are as bad as the English. This Demand is absolute robbery. We cannot AFFORD to stay in Ireland." He relapsed into gloomy silence. Ma hovere by the bedside. Buttercup came running up the stairs to see what was in the mail. "It amazes me," said the Guv, "why the Irish Tax people do not try to kcep people like us in the country instead of driving us out by excessive, savage taxation! We spend a lot here, but the Tax Office is never satisfied, they want to have their cake and eat it at the same time. We Authors are taxed more harshly than any other class over here."

I nodded sympathetically, and pushed my head against the Guv's leg. He wanted to become an Irish Citizen, he LOVED the Irish -- all except Irish Tax officials! That body, to the Guv, was a smell worse than an uncleaned tomcat tin, they were so unreasonable, so BLIND. The Guv reached out and tweaked one of my ears, "If it were not for you cats, Feef, we would go to Tangier, or Holland, or somewhere that welcomed us more.

But you are our old Granny Cat, and I would not upset you if my life depended upon it." "Phooey, Guv!" I replied, "YOU are talking! I'll stand as much as you will -- and a bit more. My heart is sound!" "Yes, Feef," he replied as he rubbed my chin and chest, "Your heart is sound, you are the nicest old Granny Cat ever." "Maybe," I answered, "You and I will pass over at the same time and then won't be parted. I'd LIKE that!"

We were all a bit gloomy for the rest of the day. Clearly it was a waste of time to try to live in Ireland if the Tax Officials were going to take all. We had enough trouble with- out that; the Press men were always snooping around, sometimes watching the house through binoculars and holding mirrors on poles to the bedroom windows. The Press had published untrue stories about the Guv and at no time allowed him to give HIS side of things. The Guv looks at Pressmen as being the scum of the Earth, I know, I have heard him say so often enough! From what Miss Ku told me I know that he is fully justified.

"I'm going up to Mrs. O'Grady's to telephone Brud Campbell," said Ma, "I see that someone has forced the lock on the back gate and it must be repaired." "Oh! I expect it was those tourists from Liverpool," replied the Guv, "Brud told me that his Father had had tourists camping in his front garden." Ma went off up the road just as Miss Ku called me from the kitchen and said that there was a very nice lunch ready for us. I went down the stairs and was met at the bottom by Miss Ku. "Here you are, Feef," she said, "I have persuaded Buttercup to give us ours early so that we can go into the garden and see if the flowers are growing all right. She groaned a bit, but did the Right Thing in the end. Tuck in!" I could always "tuck in". I LOVED food and always believed in eating in order to build up one's strength.

Now I weighed all of seven pounds and had never felt better. I found my way about without trouble, too! The Guv showed me how. "You are a silly old dope, Feef," he said. "How's that Guv?" I asked. "Well, you are blind, yet in the astral you can see. Why not, when you rest, go into the astral plane so that you can see if anything has been shifted? Why not have a jolly good look over the place. You cats don't use the brains you were born with!" The more I thought about it the more I liked it, so I cultivated the habit of astral traveling whenever I rested. Now I do not get bumps or bruises, I know the location of almost everything.

"Brud's come!" called Ma. Ku and I were delighted, it meant that now we could get in the garden, because the Guv always went out and talked to Brud Campbell and talked while he worked. We rushed to the door, and Miss Ku told the Guv he should take a tonic as he was SLOWING UP.

"Slowing up?" he replied, "I could catch you at any time!" At first the layout of the house had puzzled me because one entered by the top floor and the ground floor was below the level of the road. Miss Ku explained it to me, "Well, you see we are perched on the side of the cliff like a lot of broody hens. The cliffslopes down from the road, with a wall to keep people falling off. Anyway, this house used to be two flats until we came and knocked it into one!" We had plenty of room in the house and in the garden. There were two gardens, one at each side of the house. Formerly the upstair tenants had had the right garden and the downstair tenants the left. We had the lot. There were trees with low branches, but I was never allowed out alone because the Family always had the fear that I would fall over the cliff or climb a tree and fall off. Of course I would not have fallen, really, but it was nice to have people care that much about me.

Buttercup used to sit in the garden and sun herself, making her yellow top yellower, as Miss Ku put it. We liked her to be in the garden because she often forgot about us and we could explore more. Once I went to the side of the cliff and tried to climb down. Miss Ku very hurriedly called the Guv and he came and lifted me back before I could fall.

We had to be careful when we were out in the garden for yet another reason; people used to hang around trying to get photographs of the Lama. Cars used to stop alongside the garden walls, and people would clamber over so that they could see where Lobsang Rampa lived. One sunny afternoon the Guv looked out of a window and saw women having a picnic on the lawn! They were most annoyed where he went out and moved them off. Most residents on the scenic roads of Howth had similar experiences, trippers thought they could go anywhere, do as much damage as they wished, and leave their litter for others to clean up.

"Feef, I have just heard the Guv and Ma talking," said Miss Ku. "Where is Morocco?" "Morocco? Miss Ku, why, that will be Tangier, a place in the Mediterranean area. I was taken there by Mme. Diplomat. We nearly went to live there. It is hot, smelly, and even the fish are smugglers!"

I knew the place, all right! I had been taken there on a ship from Marseilles, and was sea-sick all the time. I had been able to see in those days, and the fierce natives in their soiled robes had frightened me quite a lot. I hoped that we would not be going to Tangier!

Miss Ku and I slept through the afternoon. The Guv and Ma had gone to Dublin and Buttercup was busily engaged in cleaning out her bedroom. We knew we should not be able to get out, so we slept and did a bit of astral travelling. Like women the world over, whether they be women cats or women humans I had FEARS. I lived in fear that I would some day wake up, and find myself in some suffocating, stinking box at an Airport. Of course, when I was awake, and heard voices, had people touch me and make a fuss of me I knew that all the bad past was indeed the past, but in sleep, one fears nightmares. Often in the night the Guv would take me in his arms and say "Now! Now! Feef, don t be such a silly old thing, OF COURSE you are home and you are going to stay with us for the rest of your life." Then I would purr and smile to myself and feel reassured. Then I would fall asleep and have nightmares all over again!

"Feef! They are back, they are driving up the hill!" Miss Ku wheeled around and raced me to the front door. We got there just in time as the car drew up. Miss Ku got in the car to help the Guv put it away and see that the garage was properly locked. Then she had to walk back along the high wall to be sure that snails were not eating away the cement!

She jumped over the green gate and yelled at the door, "Open up! Open up! We are here." Then the Guv caught up with her and opened the door and in they came.

"Well?" said Buttercup, when we were all sitting down. "How did you get on?"

"A waste of time," said the Guv.

"We went to the Moroccan Embassy but the fellow there was most unhelpful. We shall NOT be going to Tangier."

They lapsed into silence, and I purred to myself with pleasure at the thought NO Morocco. "We saw Mr. and Mrs. Vet in Dublin," said Ma. "They are coming out tomorrow to have tea with us" I felt gloomy, Mister the Irish Vet was a nice man, a very kind and pleasant man, but no vet, no matter how good, is a hero to his cat patients.

Miss Ku frowned, "Ears, Feef, ears! Let's get out of it tomorrow or we shall have our ears done." The Family went on talking discussing what to do, where to go. We wandered out of the room and down the stairs in order to get our tea.

Mister the Irish Vet arrived with Mrs. the Irish Vet. We liked him a lot, but his clothes smelled terribly of animals' insides and drug-things. Mister the Irish Vet was very interested in a big telescope the Guv used to look at far-distant ships. Miss Ku and I were hidden beneath an armchair which had a frill around it, and we listened to all that was said.

"Fifi is doing very well," said the Guv. "Ah! Sure she is," said Mister the Irish Vet. "Do you think she would stand a journey to Cork, or to Belfast?" asked the Guv. "She would indeed!" said Mister the Irish Vet, "She would stand anything so long as she knew she was wanted. She is in better health than you, anyhow!" "Hear! Hear." I muttered to myself, "All I want is to be wanted and I can stand anything." They went out into the garden and set up the big telescope. Miss Ku rushed up to hide behind the window frame so that she could see out without being seen. "They are looking at a ship, Feef," said Miss Ku. Then, suddenly, "HIDE! They are coming in!" There was the scraping of feet on the doormat and then they came in. "Have you seen the cats today?" asked the Guv. "Only their tails disappearin round the corner," said Mister the Irish Vet. "Sure an I'm proud of Fifi," he went on, "She was a very good Mother. I have been down and examined the kittens. They are doing FINE!" I started to purr with pleasure. Miss Ku hissed, "Shut up, you old fool! They will hear you!"

That night the Guv was ill, more ill than usual. Something had gone wrong inside him. I thought perhaps he had the same trouble as I had had and said so to Miss Ku. "Feef." she replied, half amused, half cross, "How could the Guv possibly have a uterine tumor? You are even more feeble minded than I thought, Feef!"

The next day he went to see Doctor, the Irish Specialist. A taxicab came to the door and off the Guv and Ma went, off down the hill, round the corner out of Miss Ku's sight and on to Dublin. Time dragged on. Time crawled slower and slower; we were worried. At last Miss Ku detected the sound of a car laboring up the hill. Gears were changed, the car speeded up, and then slowed and stopped at the door. Ma and the Guv came in, the Guv looking paler and more worn than usual, and Miss Ku hastily whispered to me. We moved aside in order not to get in the way, but the Guv -- ill or not -- always had time and energy to stoop and talk to "his children." I felt the lack of vitality in his hands as he caressed me, and I felt sick in my stomach with the worry. Slowly he went into his bedroom and went to bed.

That night Miss Ku and I took turns to stay awake with him. Yes, I know that many humans will laugh at that, thinking that "animals" have no sense, no reason, no feelings for others, but humans are animals as well! Miss Ku and I understand all and every word said or thought. We understand humans, but humans do not understand us, nor do they try to, preferring to regard us as "inferior creatures," "dumb animals," or the like. We do not make war on each other, nor do animals kill needlessly but only in order to eat. We do not torture nor put our fellows in concentration camps.

We -- Siamese Cats -- have probably the highest intelligence quotient of all animals. We feel, we love and often fear, but never hate. Humans never have the time to investigate our intelligence for they are too busy trying to make money by any fair or unfair means which presents itself. The Guv knows us as well as he knows himself. He can talk to us by telepathy as well as Miss Ku and I talk. And we can (and do!) talk to him. As the Guv says, humans and animals could talk together by telepathy in the days of long ago but Mankind abused the privilege and so lost the power.

Animals still have that power.

Days grew into weeks and the Guv did not improve. There was talk now of a Nursing Home, an operation. And all the time he grew paler and had to rest more. Miss Ku and I were very quiet, very concerned nowadays and did not press to go in the garden. We mourned in private and tried to conceal our fears from the Guv.

One morning after breakfast, when I was sitting on the bed with him and Miss Ku was in the window telling the seagulls not to make such a noise, the Guv turned to Ma and said, "Read this article. It tells of the wonderful oppor- unities in Canada. Apparently Writers, Artists, Doctors -- you think?" Ma took the article and read it. "READS all right," she said, "But I don't trust any of these articles. I thought you wanted to go to Holland? You are not well enough, anyhow!"

"We can't stay here," said the Guv, "The Irish Tax people make it impossible. Sheelagh!" he called to Buttercup. The Guv always followed the Eastern custom of consulting the whole family. "Sheelagh," he asked, "What do you think of Canada?" Buttercup looked at him as if he were not quite right in his head. Miss Ku worked overtime giving me a running commentary on the things I could not see.

"Gee!" she said in a whisper, "Buttercup thinks he is so ill he does not know what he is saying. Canada? CANADA? HO-LY!"

Later in the morning the Guv got out of bed and dressed. I could sense that he did not know what to do. Calling Miss Ku and lifting me across his shoulder he walked out into the garden. Slowly he walked down the garden path and stood looking out to sea. "I'd like to stay here for the rest of my life, cats," he said, "but the Tax men here make such extortionate demands that we HAVE to move in order to live. Would you two like to go to Canada?"

"Gee, Guv," said Miss Ku, "We will go anywhere you say:"

"Yes, I am well enough to travel," said I, "I am willing to go anywhere, but you are not well enough."

That evening the Guv had to go to Doctor, the Irish Specialist again. He returned hours later, and I could tell that the news was bad. However he still had a discussion about Canada. "The Canadian Ministry of Immigration are advertising in the papers," he said, "Let us send for some details. Where is the Embassy?" "Merrion Square," said Buttercup.

Several days later wads of advertising stuff came from the Canadians in Dublin. The Family settled down to read the whole lot. "They make a lot of promises," said the Guv.

"Yes but this is only advertising stuff," said Ma. "Why not , call at the Embassy?" asked Buttercup. "Yes," replied the Guv, "We must be very sure that the cats will be welcomed, I would not consider it if they had to go in quarantine or anything like that. Quarantine is an evil thing anyhow."

The Guv and Ma went out in the Humber and drove away to Dublin. The morning dragged on; time always drags when the future is uncertain and when loved ones are absent. At last they returned. "Red tape! Red tape!" said the Guv, "it always amazes me that such petty officials are so unpleasant. I'd like to put some of these fellows across my knee and slap their -"

"But you don't want to take any notice of them " said Ma. "They are only clerks and know no better."

Miss Ku sniggered and whispered, "The Old Man could beat 'em up and like it! His arms are far far stronger than those of Westerners, and he has had to fight a lot. Gee . I'd like to see him beat 'em up!" she sighed. The Guv WAS big, there was ample room for Miss Ku and me to sit on him together. Nearly two hundred and thirty pounds, it was all muscle and bone. I like big people, probably because I never had enough food to permit me to grow to my full size.

"We filled in all the forms, had our finger prints taken, and all that rubbish," said the Guv to Buttercup. "Tomorrow I am going to take you in to see them. You have to go as our adopted daughter. Otherwise you have to have a certain sum of money, someone to guarantee you, or some other bilge. The Canadians we have seen so far appear to be very childish." "You forgot to say that we all have to go for a medical examination", said Ma. "Yes," replied the Guv, "We will ask Mrs. O'Grady if she will stay with the cats, I'm not leaving THEM alone for anybody, they mean more to me than the whole of Canada put together." Lunch was ready, so we attended to that first, I always believed that one could discuss things more calmly after a good meal. We lived well, nothing was too good for us cats. Miss Ku was -- and is - a very small eater; she took the utmost care of her figure and she was indeed a most elegant and delightful young woman cat.

"Hey!" called the Guv, "Mrs. O'Grady is coming down the road." Ma hastened out to intercept her and bring her in. Miss Ku and I went downstairs to find out what Buttercup was doing, we hoped that she would be sitting in the garden, because then we would be able to go out and do some gardening. I had planned for some time to uproot a few plants so that I could be sure they were growing satisfactorily. Miss Ku had her mind set on looking at Mister Rabbit's house. He lived in a hole in the cliffside and often by night he came past our windows and laughed at us for being in the house. We both wanted to have a few words with him about his uncivil manner. However, it was not to be, Buttercup was doing something in her room, so we wandered along and sat in the room where we stored our cases.

The next morning was a busy one. The Guv took us out early so that we could have our say with Mister Rabbit. Miss Ku descended the cliffface about twelve feet and shouted her message through his front door. I lay across the Guv's shoulder -

- he would not let me go down -- and shouted down to Miss Ku the things I wanted to say. We were very cross at Mister Rabbit. Then we had to do our claws on one of the trees. We had to be just right so that we could look after Mrs. O'Grady when the Family were in Dublin. We each took a bath in the dust at the end of the garden, rubbing it well into our fur, then we were ready for a five-minute wild chase round the garden. I followed Miss Ku closely because in that way she guided me and I did not bump into anything. We always took the same path, so I knew all the obstacles.

"Come on in, you savages!" said the Guv. Shuffling his feet and pretending to be fierce he got Miss Ku to run as fast as she could into the house. Lifting me and slinging me across his shoulder he carried me in and shut the door after.

"Quick! QUICK! Feef," called Miss Ku, "There is a new grocery box here, it is full of news!" The Guv put me down, and I hastened to the box so that I could read of the latest news from the shop in the village.

The Family were ready to go. Tweaking our ears, the Guv said goodbye to us and told us to look after Mrs. O'Grady.

"Okay!" said Miss Ku, "She will be safe with us, should we put the chain on the door?" For a moment I thought of suggesting that Mr. Loftus should be asked to come and look . after her but then I realized that the Guv would have done that if he had considered it necessary. Mrs. O'Grady settled herself down, and Miss Ku said, "Come on, Feef, now is the time to do a few of those jobs which we can't do when the Family is here." She turned and led the way downstairs. We went round the house thoroughly to make sure that Mister Rabbit had not broken in to steal anything. Every so often Miss Ku would say, "I'll just slip upstairs and see that Ve O'G is doing all right. We simply MUST look after her." Off she would go, clattering up the stairs, deliberately making a noise so that Ve O'G would not feel spied upon. Each time Miss Ku would return and say, "Yep! She is all right" Time dragged -- worse -- time seemed to be going backwards. "Do you think they are all right, Miss Ku." I asked for the thousandth time. "Of course they are all right, I've been through things like this before. OF COURSE they are all right!" she exclaimed, trying to convince herself. Only by the nervous twitching of the tip of her tail did she betray any emotion. "You know quite well that they have to go to see a doctor all three have to be examined, and then they have to go to a hospital to have their lungs X-rayed." She nervously licked a hand, muttering 'tut-tut, tut-tut' as she surveyed her well manicured claws.

We could not face up to food. Food never took the place of love! As I fretted away I recalled my dear Mother's words to me, "Now now, Fifi," she had said, "keep calm under all circumstances. Worry never solved a single problem; if you are busy worrying you have not the time to see the way out of a difficulty." "Do you think they are all right, Feef" asked Miss Ku. "Yes, Miss Ku," I replied, "I am sure they are on the way home now." "Poor Mrs. O'Grady," said Miss Ku, "I think we should go upstairs and comfort her." We rose and made our way along the corridor, Miss Ku leading and I following in her footsteps. Together we mounted the stairs and proceeded along the upper corridor, then flung our- selves with yells of joy at the door as it opened and The Family came in.

The hospital had soon detected the Guv's scars, had soon detected that he had had T.B. and a myriad of other complaints. "I will put in a recommendation that you be permitted to go," said the hospital doctor, "for with your education and writing ability you would be an asset to Canada." More days passed, and then the Guv had a letter which said he could go to Canada if he would sign this and sign that and report to the Medical Officer of Health in Canada. The Guv was so cross about all the silly red tape that he almost tore up the papers, unfortunately (as we now think) he just signed them with a shrug of his shoulders.

"How are we going to get the cats there?" asked Ma.

"They will go with us in the plane or NONE of us will go. I'm SICK of all these fool Regulations!" said the Guv. For days they tried different airlines in an attempt to locate one which would permit us to travel with The Family instead of being in a dark and cheerless luggage hold. At last Swissair line agreed that if the Guv had The Family travel by first class, and paid BAGGAGE RATES on Miss Ku and me we could be in the first- class compartment with them, provided that we all traveled when there were many empty seats. The Guv made it clear that he was not going to be parted from us, so he paid all the many pounds demanded. Then he had another thought; we were going to fly direct to Idlewild Airport, New York instead of flying to Montreal. If a Canadian airline had taken us we should have had the shorter route across Canada, but as Swissair flew direct to New York we had no choice. The question now was, Swissair would take us in the passenger compartment, but would the American line which would have to take us from New York to Detroit? The Guv had a fear that unless everything was settled first, we would be stuck at New York without means of transport. Our affairs were being handled by a Travel Agent in Dublin, so the Guv had him make a definite enquiry of the American line, and if they agreed, book and pay first-class fares from New York to Detroit, and hire a car to take us across the American-Canadian Border to Windsor where we were going to live.

The Agent checked, and finding that the Airline in New York agreed to have us in the passenger compartment, paid all the fares. "So," he said, "there is nothing more to worry about. Now you have to take these receipts to the Embassy, show them that you have enough money to live in Canada until you find work, and that is all there is to it. Thanks for your custom. If you want to come back at any time I shall be pleased to handle it for you." Once again the Guv and Ma went to the Canadian Embassy where they showed that everything was in order. "Got a veterinarian's certificate to show that the cats are in good health?" asked a surly clerk.

"Yes!" said the Guv, producing the required papers. Now, with nothing more to complain about, the officials had to issue the necessary permission to enter Canada as a "landed immigrant." As the Guv now says, ruefully, "We were 'landed' all right!" With the papers in order, the Guv and Ma returned, tired out, to us at Howth.

"Now, Cats," said the Guv, "when we leave you will have to be in your baskets, but as soon as we are in flight you can come out and sit with us. All clear?" "All clear, Guv," said Miss Ku, "we shall want to come out, mind!" "Sure you shall come out, now stop worrying, you have cost me about your weight in gold!" Then he thought a minute and added, "and you are both worth every bit of it." Mister the Irish Vet knew some blind Irish humans who made baskets, so the Guv had a basket each made for Miss Ku and me.. Each was the absolute maximum size and gave us ample room. The Guv suggested that we use the baskets as bedrooms for a week or so in order to become accustomed to them. We did so, and it was fun!

The Guv's health worsened. By all the laws of common sense we should have given up the Canadian trip. Instead the Guv went to Doctor the Irish Specialist again and something was done whereby he could keep going. He had to rest more and more and I, knowing what it was to be ill and old, feared greatly for the outcome of it all. The Guv had had hardships and suffering in many lands and now the results of those hardships were showing. Miss Ku and I looked after him as best we could.

"How are we going to get to Shannon?" asked Buttercup.

"NOT in the Irish train," replied the Guv, "we should have to change at Limerick, and I do not feel up to that. You and Ma go to Dublin and see if you can get a garage to drive us down in a Minibus or something" "We will go down a day early," said Ma, "because you need a day's rest before going aboard the plane. It will be better for the cats, too." Off they went to Dublin, leaving Miss Ku and me to sit on the Guv in order to keep him in bed. As we all waited for Ma and Buttercup to return the Guv told us stories of cats he knew in Tibet.

"It is all arranged," said Ma, "they are willing to take us and they have a Minibus which they use for sightseeing tours. The man who will drive often goes to Shannon to meet American tourists." Now there was little to be done.

The Guv had to go yet again to Doctor the Irish Specialist. All our preparations were being kept very secret because the Press gave us no peace. I remember a short time before, when the Guv had been very ill and was going out for the first time to see the Specialist. As soon as the Guv walked out of the door, a Pressman drove up and started asking him impertinent questions. It always amazed the Guv why pressmen should think they had some sort of divine right to ask questions. "Paid gossips" the Guv called them, and he would dearly have liked to throw them over the cliff.

"Hey! Irish Rabbit!" yelled Miss Ku, some twelve feet down the cliff face. "Rabbit! We are going away so don't you wreck the garden in our absence." Mister the Irish Rabbit did not answer. Miss Ku contented herself with breathing hard down the hole and then, she rushed up to the top of the cliff again. "Birds! BIRDS!" shrieked Miss Ku, "Birds we are going to fly like you, we are going to fly further." "Hush, hush! Miss Ku," I remonstrated, "We are supposed to be keeping this a secret. Now all the birds and Mister the Irish Rabbit know." Miss Ku looked over her shoulder, and I felt her stiffen. "BOLT! Feef," she exclaimed, "Follow me Old Vet Face is coming!" We rushed indoors, out through the kitchen and into the coal cellar. "Whew!" shuddered Miss Ku,""I can almost feel my ears tingle at the thought of having them cleaned." Stealthily Miss Ku put her head round the corner, found the coast was clear, and ventured out. Voices. Voices at the head of the stairs.

"Tranquilizers," said Mister the Irish Vet. "Give them one each of these before taking them on the plane and they will rest peacefully, special tranquilizers they are." There was silence for a time, then the Guv said, doubtfully, "Will they be all right for Feef?" "Oh sure they are all right for her, all right for us too," said Mister the Irish Vet. They wandered into a room and we heard no more. Certainly we were not going to risk our ears by venturing closer and getting caught.

Mister the Irish Vet was VERY efficient at cleaning ears. Cases had been sent off to be put aboard a ship. Clothes, books, some photographic equipment, and a new electric typewriter which the Guv had bought just before deciding to emigrate. Now the luggage which we were going to take was stacked in the hall. Not much, because one could not take much by air. Miss Ku and I each took our own personal Toilet Tin, an ample supply of Peat Moss (which we used in place of earth) , and a comforting quantity of food. WE were not going to be hungry! The Guv sat talking to Mrs. O'Grady. Mr. Loftus was standing outside looking quite pale and worried. Slowly Miss Ku and I wandered through the soon-to-be-deserted house, saying farewell to loved pieces of furniture. Miss Ku jumped on to a window sill and shouted "Goodbye, Mr. Rabbit, goodbye birds."

"The bus is here!" said Ma. Willing hands took the cases and stowed them in the back of the bus. Mr. and Mrs. O'Grady tried to make jokes to lighten the parting. Dear old Mr. Loftus stood sadly by, surreptitiously wiping his eyes with the back of his hands. Slowly the Guv looked over the house to make sure nothing was left, then wearily he locked the front door and withdrew the key, passing it to Mr. O'Grady to send to the Solicitor who was going to see to the disposal of the house. Shaking hands with the O'Gradys and Mr. Loftus once again, the Guv turned away and entered the bus. The door slammed.

Slowly the bus rolled down the hill, away from the physical presence of the best friends we had in the world. We turned the corner, and started off to life.

Chapter Six

The bus rolled along the harbor road, passed under the old tram bridge, speeded up and soon left Howth Castle behind us. We were all silent, the Guv already worn and weary, looking out at the land he loved and was so reluctant to leave. "If only those Tax People were not so rapacious!" I thought. We sat by him, silent in sympathy. At Sutton we all looked to the left to give a silent farewell to another old friend, Dr. Chapman. On, on towards Dublin, with the smell of the seaweed blowing in from the mouth of the River Liffey and the seagulls calling a sad farewell overhead.

Miss Ku sat in the back on a luggage rack where she could see out, "Get a good listen at this, Feef," she called to me, sitting by the Guv. "I will give you a running commentary on the things you have never seen. This is Clontarf, we are just passing the Gardens." There was little talk in the bus, no one spoke except Miss Ku. I had had six months of Heaven in Ireland, six months in which to realize that I was wanted, that I "belonged." Now we were leaving, leaving for WHAT? The bus rolled on without jerks or starts, for the people of Ireland are very courteous and always consider the rights of the other driver.

Traffic was becoming thicker now. At times we stopped, when the lights were against us. Suddenly Miss Ku said, "We are passing Trinity College, Feef, say goodbye to it."

Trinity College! Just opposite was the Travel Agency which had made all the arrangements. I wished that I could stop in and have them all cancelled. The Guv reached down and rubbed me under my chin and pulled me closer. Traffic was thinning out as we reached the outskirts of the city. The driver speeded up.

"We are going to Limerick, Feef," said Miss Ku, "I could tell you one; There was a young cat of Kildare who had catnip flowers in her hair . . ." "Shut up, Ku!" said the Guv, "How can anyone think while you are there groaning away."

For a time all was quiet, but Miss Ku was never silent for very long. Sitting up she gave a running report of all things of interest which she thought I should know about. I am old, and have had a hard life. Trying to manage without sight is difficult. The journey tired me so I slept awhile.

Suddenly I sensed a different motion and quickly sat up Were we there? How long had I slept? What was happening?

The bus slid to a halt. "It is all right, Feef," said the Guv, "We have just stopped for tea."

"Halfway to Shannon," said the Driver, "I always stop here, they serve very good teas."

"You two go in," said the Guv, "the cats and I will stay here." "All right," said Ma, "I will bring your tea out. Ku'ei and Fifi can have theirs at the same time." Ma and Buttercup left the bus and I could hear them walking. The 'click' of a door, and they were in a shop. "Market town" said Miss Ku, "Lots of cars parked. Nice little place. People look friendly. There is an old woman smiling at you, Feef, smile back. She's blind," yelled Miss Ku to the old woman, "she can't see you, talk to me instead!" "Ah! shure," said the old woman, pressing her face close to the window, " 'tis wonnerful crayturs they are an' all. 'Tis meself the little one was talkin' to. Wonnerful what they have nowadays!" "Aw, come on, Maw! Yer've got to get Paw's tea or he'll be off to O'Shaughnesseys." "Ah! Ah! 'Tis right you are, I must be Goin' " said the old woman as she shuffled off. "I liked her shawl," said Miss Ku, "I would like to have it as a bedcover"

Ma came out bringing food and drink for the Guv. She gave us our tea, too, but we were too excited to eat much.

"What have you got, Guv?" I asked.

"Bread and butter and a cup of tea," he replied. It made me feel better to know that he was eating even a little, so I went and had a few desultory pecks at my own tea, but how CAN a cat eat when she is so excited? I thought of the travels I had had before, buffeted about in a speeding car, or drugged and half suffocated in an almost airless wooden box. NOW I was going to travel first class and not be parted from my Family. I settled down be- side the Guv and purred a little. "Old Feef is bearing up well," he said to Ma, "I think she is enjoying it even though she would not admit it!" "Say something about me!" yelled Miss Ku from the back of the bus where she was guarding the luggage and directing the Driver. "I don't know how we would manage without Ku'ei to look after us and keep us in order," the Guv said as he tweaked my ear. "Miss Ku makes more commotion than all the Cats of Kilkenny," he added.

The bus droned on, eating up the miles, taking us from all we loved and knew, to -- what? We left County Tipperary and entered County Limerick. Darkness was upon us now, and we had to go more slowly. The journey was long, long, and I wondered how the Guv would ever last. Miss Ku said he was becoming paler and paler as the miles went by.

Time meant nothing any more, hours and minutes just ran together as if we were living through eternity. The droning of the bus, the swish of the tires, the miles racing up to us, going beneath us and falling away into nothingness behind. Even Miss Ku had lapsed into silence. There was no talk now, only the sounds of the bus and the sounds of the night. Time stood still as the miles fled into the anonymity of the darkness.

Miss Ku sprang to her feet, from sound sleep to wide awareness on the instant. "Feef!" she called, "are you awake?" "Yes, Miss Ku," I replied. "Fingers of light are sweeping the sky, dusting off the clouds for the airplanes," she exclaimed. "We must be near Shannon, we must be almost there." The bus droned on, but now there was an air of expectancy, The Family sat up and took notice.

The Driver said "Five minutes more. Do you want the main entrance? Are you flying tonight?" "No," said Ma, "We are resting here tonight, all tomorrow, and leaving for New York tomorrow night."

"Then you will want the Motel," said the Driver, "they have a real smart place." He drove on a little further, made a sharp turn, and went for perhaps half a mile on an Airport road before stopping at a building on the right. Getting out, he went into the Office. "No!" he said, when he returned to the bus, "you are not booked in there, we have to go to the one near the Entrance Hall, I know where it is." Perhaps another quarter of a mile, and we drew up at yet another building. The Driver checked, and found that at last we had reached the correct building. Our luggage was carried in, or the things we would want overnight were, and the heavier things were taken straight to the Airport. "I want the Ladies' Room!" yelled Miss Ku. "Here you are, then," said Ma, showing her the special tin which she had placed in the bathroom. Gently lifting me, she carried me into the bathroom and let me feel which was my tin. Afterwards, when we sauntered out into the bedroom we felt much better. As usual, The Family had a room each. I slept with the Guv, Miss Ku slept with Ma, and poor Buttercup had to sleep alone. Miss Ku and I worked hard investigating everything and making sure that we knew all the escape routes and the exact location of all necessary facilities. Then we turned to our supper.

No cat should EVER be fussed until it has had full opportunity of investigating the room. Cats must ALWAYS know exactly where everything is. Our sight is very different from that of humans and most times we see in two dimensions instead of three. We can "stop" motion that would bewilder a human; we can alter our eyes so that we can magnify an object in much the same way as a human does when he uses a glass for that purpose. We can alter our sight so that we see clearly at a great distance, or we can see things an inch from our nose. Red is beyond us, it appears silver.

Blue light to us is as bright as sunlight. The finest print is clear to us, the smallest insect. Our eyes are not understood by humans, they are wonderful instruments and enable us to see even by infra-red light. Not my eyes, though, for I am blind. My eyes, I am told, appear to be perfect, they are of a forget-me-not blue, and they are wide open, yet they see not at all.

We all slept that night, untroubled by the drone of aircraft landing, taking off again and going far over the ocean. The next morning Ma and Buttercup went out and brought back breakfast for all of us. We lazed about, Miss Ku sat at a window and admired the dresses of women passing to and from the Airport. The Guv dressed and took us to play on the grass outside the building. I was very sure that I stayed well within reach of his hands; I was not taking any risks of getting lost now!

"Feef!" said Miss Ku, "This the Airport where you came from France?" "Yes, Miss Ku," I replied, "but I came in by the baggage entrance, I have had no experience as happy as this before. From here we flew to Dublin Airport, but of course I was unconscious." "All right, Old Woman Cat," said Miss Ku, "I will keep my eye on you and see you do the Right Thing. I'm an old hand at this sort of thing." "Thank you, Miss Ku," I replied, "I shall be MOST grateful for your guidance."

Lunch time came and Ma called us in because we had to have our food and then take a rest. With the meal over, we all lay down, Miss Ku and Ma, Buttercup alone, and the Guv and me. We rested well because we did not know how well we would sleep on the airplane. I was awakened by the Guv stroking me and saying, "Feef, you are a sleepy old thing, you and Ku'ei run round and make an appetite for tea." "Come on, Feef!" called Miss Ku, "We haven't explored the corridor, there is no one out there now, COME ON!" I jumped off the bed, scratched my ear for a moment while I thought which way to go, then found the Guv's hands guiding me to the open door. Miss Ku led the way, and we carried out our scientific investigation of the corridor and analyzed the people who had passed that way. "Let's go into the Reception Clerk," said Miss Ku, "we can show off." Many people have not seen Siamese Cats, and I must admit at the risk of appearing immodest that we were a sensation. I was flattered beyond measure when people thought that I was Miss Ku's mother! We made our rounds of the Reception Office and then returned to our rooms for another sleep.

Lights all over the Airport were a twinkle when we rose again and had our supper. The gathering darkness deepened and changed to night. Slowly we gathered up our belongings, went out into the warm Irish night, and made our way across the road to the Airport. Men took our luggage and put them ready for Customs inspection. The Guv always had the kindest words for the Irish Customs men, there was NEVER any trouble with them. Our only trouble with Irish officials was with the Tax men and their greed was driving us from Ireland.

A very courteous Swissair man came and greeted us and spoke a word to Miss Ku and me.

"The Company would like you to have dinner as their guests," he said politely to The Family. "No, thank you," replied the Guv, "We have had our dinner, and we would not leave our cats even that long."

The man told us to say if there was anything he could do for us, and then he went away, leaving us alone. Ma said, "Shall we give the cats the tranquilizers?" "Not yet," said the Guv, "and I am not giving Feef any, she is always quiet. We will see how Ku is when we get aboard."

Being blind, I find that I am under a great handicap when I try to describe the next sequence of events. Miss Ku, after much persuasion and at much inconvenience to herself, has agreed to write the next few pages. . .

Well, there we were, sitting like a lot of creeps in the Main Hall at Shannon Airport. Crowds of people were sitting there like broody hens. Children were yelling their bad-tempered heads off and making mine ache with the clamor. Some Yank guys were sitting in a corner looking like a lot of stuffed ducks. They thought they were Big Wheels because they had CD bags labeled for Paris -- where the Old Woman Cat came from. The Airport clock was rusty or something, because time went slowly. At last some guy all dressed up in blue and brass came over to us and almost kissed the dust on the ground as he told us that the Swissair Flight from Shannon to New York International Airport was ready. I thought how silly, because how was it a flight when it was still on the ground. He tried to grab my basket, but the Guv and Ma weren't having any. The Guv hoisted the Old Woman Cat's basket and Ma grabbed the one I had.

Buttercup -- goodness only knows what she grabbed, I was too busy to look. Off we went, like a Sunday School party, across the floor of the Main Hall and out into the darkness that wasn't. It would have been, but every light in Shannon seemed to be shining. Out on the runway there were all kinds of colored lights. Other lights waved like fingers in the sky.

Then I looked forward and saw the plane. My! It was big, bigger than anything we had seen at Dublin Airport. It looked to me almost as big as Howth on wheels. We trailed along, getting closer and closer to that airplane, and it seemed to get bigger and bigger. At the front end there was a ladder thing with sides to it so that men on the ground could not see what we cats can always see. Women, I mean.

The Old Man carrying the Old Woman Cat climbed slowly up that ladder or stairway or whatever they call it. A well fed Purser (my! I bet he ate well!) bowed so low he almost creaked. An even better fed Stewardess dressed in navy blue and with a white collar greeted us. She did not bow, her girdle prevented her. All Stewardesses and Hostesses wear girdles, I know that from a book the Guv wrote some time ago. Anyhow they got us all in the First Class compartment, and then went to get the bread-andbutter passengers aboard. They were quartered where the noise came from.

A light thing came on to say we must not smoke (who ever heard of a cat smoking, anyhow?) and must fasten our safety belts. We did. The Guv held on to his basket as if it were precious. Ma held on to mine knowing that I was. A whacking great metal door slammed and the whole plane shook as if it would fall to pieces. However it did not, but slowly moved along past a lot of lights. Crowds of people outside waved. We saw their mouths open as they yelled. They looked just like fish we had had in a tank some time before.

We rumbled on, making a horrid noise, then when I thought we had driven nearly to America the whole thing swiveled around, almost pitching me on my ear, and the noise increased. I yelled for the Pilot to stop it, but he could not hear me for all the noise he was making. There was a sudden sensation of violent speed, so suddenly that it almost mixed my lunch with my dinner, and then we were in the air. The Pilot must have been inexperienced, because he turned the plane on its side and circled the Airport to make sure that he really had left. I saw lights below me, hundreds of the things, then I saw a lot of water glinting in the moonlight. "Hey!" I shouted to him, "that's water down there, we shall drown if we fall in!" He must have heard me because he put the plane the right way up and pointed the thing at America.

We climbed higher and higher, up through scattered clouds which were painted silver by the moonlight, up and higher yet. We went faster and faster and higher and higher and I looked out of the window and saw flames shooting behind the wings. "Golly!" I said to myself, "now they have failed to drown us they are going to fry us!" I called to the Guv and he told me it was okay (that's American for all right) and I should not worry. I looked some more and saw some pipes in the engine were white hot. I felt that way myself. The Pilot must have got my thoughts because he spoke from the ceiling and in his spiel said not to worry any, we always went up in flames while gaining height.

The fat Stewardess came over, I missed what she said because I was so alarmed at the creaks when she bent. "Her clothes will never stand it," I thought. Couple of silly Yanks lounged about in the First. Apart from them, what fat hunks they were, we were on our own. We got up to about thirty thousand feet or so, near Heaven I guess, and then the plane leveled out and we went sailing along by the stars.

"I'm going to give Ku a tablet," said Ma, slipping a, noxious substance between my lips before I or the Old Man could object. I blinked and swallowed. For moments nothing happened, then I felt a delicious lightheadedness stealing over me. The urge to sing was irresistible. Man! I sure was high! The Old Folks got madder and madder as I got happier and happier.

Special note for cat fans; the Old Man made enquiries at Detroit Zoo later and found that cats are not tranquilized by tranquilizers. IT JUST MAKES US DRUNK! Fellow at the Detroit Zoo said he had had the same experience as the Guv with a drunken cat. Well, it was fun while it lasted. Now I guess I have done my share and will pass the task back to the Old Woman Cat, after all she started it and it is her pigeon.

The plane droned on covering hundreds of miles each hour. The lights had been dimmed, and then finally replaced by a faint blue light. Miss Ku lay in her basket, laughing softly to herself. Chuckle after chuckle escaped her.

At last I could bear it no longer, curiosity overcame manners. "Miss Ku," I said softly, so as not to disturb anyone, "Miss Ku, what are you laughing about?" "Eh? Me laughin'? Oh yeah, HA! HA! HA!" I smiled to myself, Miss Ku really was "lit up" as the humans say. I had only once before seen a cat in that state, and that had been a Tom who made a practice of going into a wine cellar and drinking up the wine droppings. Now Miss Ku was like it. "Feef!" she giggled, "It's too good to keep to myself, Feef, are you listening?. FEEF".

"Yes, Miss Ku," I responded, "certainly I am listening, I shall be delighted to hear your tale." "Well," she started, "it happened just before you came to Howth. The Guv is a Buddhist Priest, or Lama, you know. He was sitting on a rock by the side of the water one day, and a young Catholic monk who was on holiday with a whole party of them sat down by the Guv. 'My son' said the monk (the Guv was old enough to be his grandfather!) 'My son, you have not been to Mass today.' 'No Father' said the Guv politely, 'I have not.' 'You must go to Mass, my son,' said the young monk, 'promise me that you will go today!' 'No, Father,' replied the Guv, 'I cannot promise you that.' 'Then you are not a good Christian, my son,' angrily retorted the young monk. 'No, Father,' answered the Guv mildly, 'I am a Buddhist Priest, an Abbot actually!' " Miss Ku stopped for a moment and then broke into peals of laughter. "Feef!" she said at last, "Feef, you should have seen that young monk, he ran off as if the devil was after him!" At last even Miss Ku became tired of talking and laughing and fell asleep. I turned in my basket, and the Guv put his hand in and rubbed my chin. With a purr I dropped off to sleep.

The Guv was ill when I awoke, the Purser was bending over him giving him some drug. The Guv is old and has had many trials and ills, on the plane he had a heart attack and I did not really expect him to survive the journey. However he said to me before we started out, "If you can stand it, Feef, I can! That is a challenge to you!" I had a special feeling for the Guv, a very special feeling, because he and I can talk together as easily as Miss Ku and I can.

"HO-LY!" said Miss Ku in gloomy tones, "I sure have got a hangover! I'd like to give Old Vet-Face some of his tranquilizers so that he could know what they are like. What do human vets know about cats, anyhow?" "What time is it please, Miss Ku?" I asked. "Time? Eh? Oh! I don't know, I'm all mixed up with the time. Anyhow, the blue light is off and the full lights are on. Soon be chow time for Them." I became aware of the clattering of dishes, and the small sounds that people make when they are waking up. I had become almost used to blindness, but it WAS frustrating not to know what was going on, not to be able to see what was happening. The Guv's hand came down to caress me. "Silly Old Woman Cat," he said, "What are you worrying about now? Wake up, it is breakfast time, and we shall very soon be landing ."

A voice in the ceiling burst into crackling life. "Fasten your seat belts, please, we are landing at New York International Airport." I heard the clink of metal, then the Guv took firm hold of my basket. The nose of the plane dropped and the engine note changed. There was a sensation of drifting, floating, then the engines came on at full power. A bump and a screech of tires. Another small bump, and the plane rumbled along the runway. "Keep your seats, please," said the Stewardess, "Wait until the aircraft comes to a standstill." We rumbled along, with the occasional squeal of brakes as the Pilot steered and checked our speed. A final drag and we slid to a standstill. The engines slowed and stopped. For a moment there was only the sound of people breathing, then a loud BUMP came from outside, followed by the scraping of metal upon metal. A door clanged open and a rush of freezing air came in. "Goodbye," said the Purser, "fly with us again!" "Goodbye," said the Stewardess, "we hope to have you with us again!"

We went down the landing ramp with the Guv carrying me, Ma carrying Miss Ku and Buttercup bringing up the rear. It was bitterly cold and I could not understand it.

"Brrr!" said Miss Ku disgustedly, "A ***** hangover and now * * * * snow!" The Family hurried along so that we should not be out in the cold a moment longer than necessary.

Soon we entered a huge hall. Miss Ku, who knew everything, said that it was the Immigration and Customs Hall and was the largest building of its type in the world. The Guv produced all our papers and we all passed through Immigration and went on to Customs. "Wafyergot?" asked a man's voice. "Nothing to declare," said the Guv, "we are in transit to Canada." "What's them, cats?" asked the Customs man. "Ahhh!" said a Customs woman, with a drooly sigh, "I've seen 'em before. BE-U-TIFUL!!" We passed on, by the difference in smell I knew that a colored man was carrying our cases, but the Guv and Ma still held on to me and Miss Ku. In the Main Entrance Hall the Guv sat down, because he was so ill, and Ma went off to see the American airline people who were going to fly us to Detroit.

She was gone a very long time. When she came back she was seething with annoyance. "They have broken their contract!" she said, "They won't have the cats in the passenger compartment, they say they must be put in the luggage hold, it is something to do with their rules and regulations. They said that a mistake was made by the Shannon people." I suddenly felt my age, felt very old. I did not feel ABLE to survive in the luggage compartment; I had had too much of that, and I was shocked that ANYONE would expect Miss Ku to endure it. The Guv said, "If the cats can't go -- we won't either! Go back and tell them we will make the biggest fuss ever, and shall claim our money back as they agreed to take the cats with us if we paid in advance." Ma went off again, and again we all settled down to wait. Eventually Ma returned and said, "I have told them you are ill, they are having us sent to La Guardia by special car. They suggest we stay at the big Motel there and then see if the Airline will change their mind."

Soon we were in a huge car, an immense Cadillac which even had air conditioning. "My!" said Buttercup, as we threaded our way through the intense New York Freeway traffic, "I should not like to drive here!" "Its all right if you keep in your own lane, Ma'am," said the Driver. Twenty minutes later we drew up at what Miss Ku told me was the biggest Motel she had ever seen. We all went in. "Do you object to having Siamese Cats here?" asked the Guv. "Sure they are welcome!" said the man at the Reception Desk taking a good look at us. "Sure they are VERY welcome," he repeated, allotting us rooms. We seemed to be carried MILES along corridors before we reached our rooms. "Ladies Room QUICK!" yelled Miss Ku. I was grateful for her remark! The necessary facilities were speedily produced, and I did much to contribute to our comfort and peace of mind.

"Food," said Ma. "See to the cats first," replied the Guv. Our routine had been very upset, but we felt that we could take it. We wandered around, looking in the three rooms we had taken, and very cautiously investigating the corridor.

"I can see the Airport," said Miss Ku, "that must be La Guardia." Ma stood up, "Well!" she said, "I will go across to the Airline and see what can be done." The door closed behind her and Miss Ku and I settled down to keep watch on the Guv. The journey had proved too much for his heart and he was flat upon a bed. Buttercup came in, "How will we get to Windsor if the Airline will not take us?" she asked.

"Don't know, maybe by train," said the Guv, "we could have a Sitting Room on a train and the cats would be with us," he added. I was dozing when Ma came back. "They won't take us unless the cats go in the luggage hold," she said.

"NO!" replied the Guv, "we will find some other way." For a long time there was silence. Miss Ku and I sitting together, both dreading that we should have to go in the luggage compartment; after all, we could not stay at the Motel long, the prices were fantastic. "They could only suggest an air taxi, said Ma. "Well," replied the Guv, "we shall get our fares refunded from La Guardia to Detroit as the Airline broke its contract. That will reduce the cost. Did they say what it would cost to fly all of us from here to Canada?" Ma told him what they estimated it would cost and he almost collapsed with the shock. So did Miss Ku and I. Then he said, "Book the plane for tomorrow morning, but it must be big enough to have the cats in with us." Ma nodded her agreement and went out once more.

Miss Ku and I exercised by racing round the rooms. As they were strange rooms Miss Ku told me where everything was and ran ahead of me, I followed her closely and we managed to have real fun and entertain the Guv at the same time, he loved to see us play and leap into the air. When we were tired Miss Ku led me to a window and told me about the tall towers of Manhattan among which the Guv had lived and worked some years before.

Ma came back and told us that everything was fixed, and that we should be in Windsor, Canada, tomorrow at this time. Then we settled down to our tea, after which we sat and thought about the new land to which we were going.

Darkness came early and we all went to our beds to get as much rest as possible; the trip from Howth had been even more tiring than we had anticipated. It was quite a pleasant Motel, but very expensive, being so close to the Airport and New York, but the Guv would never have been able to stand the journey without a rest. In the morning we had our breakfast and said goodbye to the man at the Reception Desk, he quite liked Miss Ku and me which Miss Ku said showed good sense on his part. Because the Guv was ill, and because of our luggage, we had a car provided by the Motel take us across the road and along to the office of the Air Taxi company. A very pleasant colored man drove us and went to considerable trouble making sure we reached the right office and got as close to it as we possibly could. "Ah'll wait heah, Suh," he said to the Guv, "until Ah sees you all is fixed up."

We went into the Office and at first no one seemed to know anything about us. Then a dim light appeared to glow in one man's mind and he reached for a telephone. "Sure! Sure!" he said, "the Pilot is coming over here now. Just wait there." We waited and then waited some more. Eventually a man swung impatiently into the Office and said, "You the folks going to Canada?" We said we were, Miss Ku and I adding our voices to give emphasis. "O-kay!" he said, "we will get your luggage aboard, what about them cats?"

"THEY GO IN THE PLANE WITH US!" said the Guv very firmly. "Okay," said the Pilot, "the two dames must sit in back with a basket on their knees." He led the way to the plane. "Holy!!" exclaimed Miss Ku in an awed voice, "It is nothing but a * * * * * toy! Two engines, three seater plus pilot, four in all. Three wheel undercarriage. HO-LY!" she exclaimed with even more fervor. "I don't know how we are going to get the Guv's behind in that small front seat.

Why," she roared, "even the pilot has had his head shaved in order to make more room!"

Ma and Buttercup climbed in the plane which, according to Miss Ku, had almost as much room inside as a small car, with room on the back seats for two average people. Ma is comfortably padded, Buttercup is slender, so they made two, average people. I felt the whole plane sway when the Guv got aboard. He weighed about two hundred and twenty five or two hundred and thirty pounds (he may have lost a pound or two on the trip) and the plane tipped a bit. The pilot must have been the smallest pilot of the litter, because his weight apparently had no effect. He started up the engines one after the other, and let them warm up, then letting off his brakes he taxied slowly along.

We covered miles on the ground, going to the far end of the Airport. Miss Ku gave me a running commentary. "Jeepers!" she cried, "all the aeroplanes in America are taking off from here; one a minute at least."

Suddenly the Pilot uttered a VERY naughty word and violently swung the plane sideways and off the main runway.

"We gotta flat," he growled, "Pilot of that liner just radioed me." Behind us came the ear-splitting shriek of sirens and the roar of racing engines. A whole cavalcade of cars swung off the runway and surrounded us. "My oh my!" yelled Miss Ku above the noise, "they have called out the National Guard!" She peered cautiously over the bottom of the window, ears flat so that she would not be seen. "Cops, a lot of cops out there, the fire brigade, and a carload of airport officials, and they have a breakdown truck as well. HO-LY!"

"Good Grief!" exclaimed the Guv, "What a shocking commotion for one poor little flat tire." Men were running everywhere, sirens were emitting their last dying wails, and the sound of car engines mingled with that of airliners racing up before take-off. Sudden heavy thuds and heaves beneath us, and the plane was lifted inches off the ground so that the faulty wheel could be removed. The cars raced away, then the breakdown truck dashed off with our offending wheel.

We sat back to wait. We waited an hour, two hours. "We could have WALKED to Canada in the time!" said the Guv in utter disgust. Leisurely the truck came ambling back along the service road flanking the runway. Leisurely, no, LANGUIDLY, men eased themselves out of the truck and strolled across to our plane. Eventually the wheel was fixed on again and the truck trickled off. The Pilot restarted his engines and let them warm. Talking into his microphone to the Control Tower he said that he was ready to take off. At last permission was given, and he opened the two throttles, raced the plane down the runway, and eased it slowly into the air. Climbing slowly, keeping well below the airline routes, the Pilot settled the plane on the correct bearing and put the throttles on cruising speed.

We flew and we flew and we flew, but we did not seem to be getting anywhere. "What speed are we doing, Miss Ku?" I asked. She craned her neck, looking over the Pilot's shoulder. "A hundred and twenty five, altitude six thousand feet, compass bearing North-West," replied Miss Ku. I envied her her knowledge, her ability to see. I could only sit, depending upon others to tell me things. I thought, though, of all the flights I had made shut in a box, unconscious. This was FAR better, now I was being treated BETTER than humans for I was sitting on Ma's lap.

Living with the Lama

Chapter Seven

"NOK! NOK!" said Miss Ku, peering between the Pilot's and the Guv's shoulders. "NOK! NOK! NOK! We need a parachute, Feef, THE FUEL GAUGE IS KNOCKING AGAINST THE STOP!" The Guv turned towards the Pilot. "Petrol gauge wrong?" he asked. "Out of gas," said the Pilot, casually, "we can always come down." Beneath our small wings spread the snow-covered tips of the Allegheny Mountains in Pennsylvania. Miss Ku made chills of horror race up and down my spine as she told me of the gaping chasms and the razor-backed ridges just waiting to scrape us out of the sky. The Pilot consulted his map and made a slight alteration to our course. "OW! Miss Ku" I exclaimed in fright, "we are GOING DOWN!" "Aw, keep your silly head calm," retorted Miss Ku calmly. "we are going to land and take on some petrol, there is a small airdrome just ahead of us. Now you just sink your claws in the basket and HANG ON!"

"Bump!" went the plane, "BUMP, bump!" it went again. We slithered sideways a bit on the snow, and then rolled forward along the runway. Breaking to a stop, the Pilot flung open the door, letting freezing air in. Jumping to the ground, he yelled to a woman by the petrol pump, "Fill'er up!" he commanded as he dashed for the nearest Comfort Station. The woman came over and poured a lot of petrol into the wings, not even glancing in our direction. The airdrome was shrouded in snow, covering the buildings and the runways. Miss Ku described for me the numerous small planes shackled to the ground waiting for their Owners to let them free to fly. All around the airdrome the snow covered slopes of the mountain range lay in wait for the unwary. The Guv stepped out on to the snowy wastes without a coat. "Be careful!" I called after him, "you will catch a chill!" "Don't be a dope, Feef," said Miss Ku, "this freezing weather is a heatwave to what the Guv is normally accustomed. In Tibet, where he comes from, the cold is so intense that even one's words freeze and fall to the ground!"

The engines roared again and we moved out across the rutted snow. No control tower here, in a little place like this, so the Pilot warmed his engines, opened the throttles further and raced away down the white runway. Climbing, he circled the little airdrome until he had sufficient height, and then headed across the mountains in the direction of Cleveland. By now we had had thrumming engines for so long that we no longer noticed them.

On we flew, rising and falling gently to the vagrant currents, flying on endlessly into the fading afternoon. The smoke of Pittsburgh passed away beneath our left wingtip, the haze of Cleveland loomed up ahead. "We will fly over Cleveland," said the Pilot, "and cross Lake Erie from Sandusky. Then we shall have three islands beneath us in case of engine failure." The plane droned on, the two engines singing the same monotonous song, the Pilot hunched over the controls. We had numb behinds with sitting so long. I shifted uncomfortably as the plane made a sudden turn to the right. "Great Jumping Tomcats!" exclaimed Miss "someone has upset the refrigerator and spilled all the ice cubes!" She tittered in an embarrassed manner, and said,

"It is not ice cubes really, although it looks so from this height. The whole Lake is frozen and mountains of ice are piled everywhere. From here they look like spilled ice cubes," she added self-consciously.

Beneath us the ice grated and ground together, and any clear stretch of water instantly froze solid. This, the Pilot had said, was an exceptionally cold winter and the forecast was colder yet. "Pelee Island," said the Pilot, "we are exactly halfway across the Lake. We pass over Kingsville and on to Windsor." The plane was pitching somewhat now, air being cooled by the ice, caused some turbulence. I was tired and hungry, and I felt as if I had been traveling for ever. Then I thought of the Guv, desperately ill and old. HE was bearing up, so could I. I squared my shoulders, settled myself more firmly and felt better! "Five minutes and we shall land at Windsor Airport," said the Pilot. "Ohhh!" squeaked Miss Ku in high excitement, "I can see the skyscrapers of Detroit!"

The plane banked and turned into land. The engine note changed and the plane flattened out. A gentle 'scrunch' on the snow-covered runway, and we were down, in Canada. The plane rolled gently along and turned right. "LEFT! LEFT!" said the Guv, who knew the Airport well, "that is the disused Airport, you have to go to the New one." Just then the Control Tower people spoke to the Pilot on the radio and confirmed what the Guv had just told him. The Pilot speeded up his right engine to turn the plane, moved along perhaps a quarter of a mile, and then put on the brakes and switched off the engines.

For a moment we sat still, feeling so cramped that we wondered if we would ever be able to get out. Miss Ku muttered, "As white as the top of a Christmas cake. Where did all the stuff come from?" The Pilot pushed open a door and started to get out. Suddenly, harshly, a voice bawled, "Where ya bawn, folks?" The raucous yelling of the man shocked me and I wondered what sort of a place it was. Now I know that they all speak in that rough way here. The Guv says they think they are still in the Wild West stage where courtesy and culture are considered "sissy".

The Guv replied that we were Immigrants and we had all our papers in order. The man yelled "It is after hours, Immigration is closed," before turning away and entering the Airport building. Slowly, stiffly, we got out of the plane and made for a door marked "Canada Customs." Passing through we found we were in a large, empty Hall. I knew it was large and empty by the echoes which came back from our footfalls. We walked on until we came to a counter. The man was behind it. "You are too late," he said, "you did not tell us that you were coming. No Immigration Officer here now, I can't touch your stuff until you have been cleared by Immigration." "You were notified," said the Pilot, "we notified you from La Guardia, New York, yesterday. And what about me? I have got to get back, will you sign this paper for me, it is only clearance to say that I reported to Canada Customs." The Customs man sighed so much that his uniform creaked and strained. "I shouldn't do this really," he said, "because I go off duty in a few minutes. However. . . ." His pen scratched on paper, the Pilot muttered "Thanks" to the Customs man and "Goodbye folks," to us and he was gone from our life. The engines of his plane raced up and died away in the distance.

A door opened and closed. Heavy footsteps came closer, and closer. "Hey," said the Customs man to his relief, "these folks say they are Immigrants. What are we going to do? It is after hours -- well, it is YOUR problem, I'm off duty as of now." He turned without another word and walked off. The relief man spoke in a good old Irish voice. "Sure an' we'll get you cleared. I'll get an Immigration Officer to come from the Tunnel. He turned to a telephone and soon gave an outline of the "troubles afflicting him." He turned back to us and said, "An Officer is coming, I cannot touch your stuff until he clears you as Landed Immigrants. Immigration first, then back to me at Customs. What have you got there?" he asked. "Two Siamese Cats," replied the Guv, "here are their papers providing they are in good health." The man sighed and turned to the telephone. ". . . yeah, two cats. Siamese. Yeah, I seen their papers, Yeah, only I thought maybe you would want to see them. No? Okay!" Back he came to us. "Cats can go through all right, now we gotta wait for you." Miss Ku sniggered and whispered to me, "WE are, cleared, Feef, but The Family are stuck!"

We waited and waited. Waited, so we thought, almost long enough to fly back. The Airport was deathly dull, hardly a sound rippled the silence. I sensed that the Guv was becoming sicker and sicker. Ma wandered around restlessly, and Buttercup breathed as if she were on the verge of exhaustion and sleep. Somewhere a door slammed. "Ah!" said the Customs man, "here he comes." Footsteps sounded along the corridor, two men walking. They came closer and closer.

"These folks claim they are Immigrants," said the Customs man. "I called you because I cannot touch their stuff until you have cleared them. The cats have been cleared by Health". The Immigration Officer was a nice old man, but he did not appear to know the Airport at all, nor did he know which office to enter; he kept asking the Customs man things.

Eventually he said, "Come this way," and walked off to a little side room. "Before we can start we must have Forms and things," he muttered to himself, tugging aimlessly at locked drawers. "Wait here," he said, "I must try to find some keys." He went out and soon returned with the Customs man. Together they went round trying drawers and closet doors, muttering to themselves as they found each one locked. Both men went out and we settled down to another long wait.

"Got them! Got the keys!" said the Immigration man in great triumph, "NOW we shan't be long." For minutes he tried key after key, becoming more and more gloomy. None of them fitted. Off he rushed to solicit the aid of the Customs man. Together they advanced on the offending desk. "You lift up," said the Immigration man, "and I will bear down, if we can get this in between we can force it open." The sounds of groans and grunts almost lulled us to sleep, then came the splintering of wood and the sound of a screw or two dropping to the floor from the shattered lock. For a moment no one spoke, then the Immigration man said, in a strangled voice, "The ***** desk is empty!" He and the Customs Officer wandered round, experimentally poking and pulling at desks and closets. Much MUCH later the Immigration man exclaimed, "Ah! GOT IT!" There was the rustling of papers and muttered imprecations, then a muffled voice said, "Now we have the Forms -- WHERE ARE THE RUBBER STAMPS?" More searchings, more muttered words, more waiting. Miss Ku and I settled down into a doze from which we were awakened by having our baskets lifted. "Now you go back to Customs, that is where you came in," said the Immigration man. We clattered back along the Hall. "All clear?" asked the Customs Officer, inspecting our papers now marked "Landed Immigrant." Wearily the Guv lifted cases and put them on the counter, unlocked them and opened them for inspection. Methodically the Customs Officer checked our list of cases, and glanced through our effects. "All right," he said, "you can go."

Outside the Airport the snow lay thickly, "Coldest winter for a long time," an Airport cleaner told us. Quickly our cases were stowed in a waiting car, Ma, Buttercup, Miss Ku and I got in the back. The Guv sat in the front with the driver. Off we went along the slippery road. The driver did not seem to be at all sure of the way and kept muttering to himself, "We turn here, no, it is further on, no it must be here." The ride was uncomfortable and very long. To us it seemed almost far enough for an air journey. We jolted along a terribly bad road and swerved uncertainly to a stop. "Here it is," said the car driver, "this is the house." We climbed out and carried our cases in. Miss Ku and I were really too tired to carry out a thorough inspection, so we tottered round trying to note the most important points. The Guv lifted me on to his bed, and I fell sound asleep.

With the coming of the morning Miss Ku came and awakened me, saying, "Come on, you lazy old wretch! We got work to do, now you walk behind me and I will tell you all about everything." I jumped off the bed and had a good scratch in order to wake myself up. Then I followed Miss Ku.

"Here is where we eat," she said, "and here is the Comfort station. Here is a wall against which you would dash your brains if you had any. Now note its position for I shall not repeat myself!" She went on, "Here is a door, it leads to a small garden with a garage at the end and the road beyond that." She led me through the house and jumped on to a window ledge in the Guv's bedroom. "Gee! Feef!" she exclaimed, "There is a sun porch outside, and then a big lawn and beyond that the sea. The sea is frozen." "Don't be such a dope, Ku, said the Guv lifting me to his shoulder, Come on, Ku," he called, moving to the other door. Opening it, he carried me through, and Miss Ku rushed past to be 'out first.' "That is not the sea," said the Guv, "it is Lake St. Clair, and when the weather is warmer you can both go out and play on the grass."

It was a strange kind of house, a grating in the ceiling of each downstair room allowed hot air to go to the room above. Miss Ku LOVED to sit in an upstair bedroom right on a grating, and watch what was going on in the kitchen below. She got extra heat from that rising from the kitchen stove, but it had the great attraction of enabling her to know all that was going on, in the kitchen, tradesmen at the door, and what was being said in the Guv's bedroom.

A few days after we arrived in Canada it was Christmas. It was quiet indeed, we knew no one at all, and during the whole of what was for others "the Festivities" we saw no other person, nor spoke to anyone. The weather was bitter, with constant snowfalls, and the surface of the Lake was a solid sheet of ice upon which ice yachts sped. I thought of the other years and of other Christmases. Mme. Diplomat had been an ardent Catholic, and "Noel" had meant much to her. The LAST Christmas, I recalled, I had been shut up in that dark old shed, shut up for the whole of the day after, too. Because of the celebrations they had forgotten all about me.

THIS Christmas was truly the happiest ever, because I could look back along the years and know that now I was truly wanted, and know that no longer would I be lonely or forgotten, or hungry. In my "Mme. Diplomat" days I remained hidden as much as possible. Now, if I am missing for even a few minutes someone says, "Where is Feef? Is she all right?" and a search is immediately instituted. NOW I have learned that I am wanted, so I keep in sight, or make my presence known as soon as my name is mentioned. Food too is regular; the Guv says I eat one meal a day -- all day! He does not believe in feeding animals just once a day. He thinks that we have sense enough to know when we have had enough. Consequently Miss Ku and I always have food and drink available, day and night.

Christmas was past, and we were feeling the remoteness of our rented home from the shops. No bus passed our door, and the city was about fifteen miles away. The only way to get anywhere was by taxi. Delivery men came to the door, bringing milk, meat and bread, but there was no real CHOICE.

The Guv decided to buy a car. "We will get an old one first," he said, "and when we get used to the wild Canadian drivers we will get a better one." One thing that impressed the Guv was the utter lack of courtesy on the roads. As he often said, The Americans were probably the world's worst drivers, with the Canadians a very close second. As the Guv has driven in some sixty countries he should know something about it.

The taxi drew up at the door and the driver hooted. The Guv went out. Miss Ku called after him, "Get a good car, Guv, don't let them swindle you!" I heard the taxi door slam and the sound of a car driving off. "Hope he gets a good one," said Miss Ku, "I LOVE car driving, I simply can't wait to get out in it." It was perfectly true, Miss Ku would ride anywhere at any time and she loved speed. I dislike car riding unless I can go at not more than twenty miles an hour. There is no fun in speed when one is blind. Miss Ku prefers to race along the highway going at least the maximum allowed by the law. The morning passed slowly, we cats fretting at being without the Guv and Ma. Miss Ku's ears went up, "They are coming, Feef," she said, I listened, and then I heard it. Unfortunately it was a taxi returning! Buttercup ran down the stairs and hurried to the door. Miss Ku jumped on the window ledge and uttered an exclamation of disgust. "They have come back by taxi, they haven't bought a car!" she said, irritably.

Buttercup opened the door, "Well? How did you get on?" she asked. Miss Ku yelled, "QUEEK! QUEEK! Spill the beans, GIVE! What happened?" "Well," said the Guv, "we saw a car which appeared to be very suitable. It is an old Monarch. The firm are going to send it out here so that we can try it for the day. If we like it we pay for it and keep it."

Miss Ku turned and raced up the stairs, her tail fluffed with joy. "I'll go up and keep watch through the bathroom window," she shouted. The Guv and Ma told Buttercup and me all that had happened. We were just going to have a cup of tea when Miss Ku shouted, "It is coming, two cars, YIPPEE!" I could hear her doing a little dance of joy in the room above. The Guv and Ma went out and Miss Ku got in a fever of impatience, rushing around like a cat who had just had her kittens taken from her. "Golly! Golly!" she breathed,

"What CAN they be doing?" Buttercup could not bear the suspense either. Putting on her thickest coat she dashed out.

Miss Ku emitted an ear-splitting yowl, "I can see it, Feef! It is green and as big as a bus!" The Family came in just in time to save Miss Ku from bursting with frustration. The Guv looked at her, then picked her up and said, "So you want to see the car, eh? Do you want to come, Feef?" "No thank you," said I, "just leave me here where it is safe!" The Guv, carrying Miss Ku, and Buttercup -- well wrapped up -- went out into the cold air. I heard the sound of an engine. Ma rubbed my head and said, "You will be able to go for rides, now, Feef."

Half an hour later they came back. Miss Ku was bubbling with excitement. "Wonderful WONDERFUL!" she yelled at me. "I went to Tecumseh." "Miss Ku," I said, "you will throw a fit if you go on like that. Why not sit here and tell me all about it, I can't follow you when you stutter and stammer with excitement." For a moment I thought she was going to be angry, then she came across and sat by the space heater.

Folding her hands primly, she said, "Well, it was like this Feef." The Old Man carried me out and put me on the back seat. He got in the driving seat, and there was plenty of room for him -- you know what a lot of room he takes. Buttercup sat in the front passenger seat and the Guv started the engine.

Oh! I must tell you this; the car is green and is an automatic, whatever that means, and there is room for all of us and two others. The Guv drove slowly, he is too law abiding -- I told him so, and he said wait until we have paid for the thing. And they are going to drive over and pay the money this afternoon and then we can go fast. So we drove to Tecumseh and then we came back, so here we are!" She paused a moment while she combed the end of her tail, and said, "You should see it, Feef! Oh! I forgot you are blind, well, you should get your behind on those seats. Be-Utiful!" I smiled to myself, Miss Ku was really thrilled by the car. I was thrilled to know that now the Guv would be able to get out a little. "Feef!" said Miss Ku, "The car is WARM, Gee! You could fry eggs in it if you wanted to."

Lunch was soon over, then the Guv and Ma got ready to go out. "We shan't be long, said Ma, "we are just going to pay for the car and get some groceries, We'll give you a ride when we come back." "I wouldn't want to go out Miss Ku" I said, "I am not fond of cars."

"Oh! you are a silly old woman cat!" said Miss Ku. She sat up and went thoroughly into her toilet, ears, back of her neck, whole body, and right on to the tip of her tail. "I have to make a good impression on the new car," she explained, "or it may not run well if it dislikes me." Surprisingly quickly the Guv and Ma came back. I was delighted to hear the rustle of brown paper and thus to know that a fresh supply of food had been laid in. One of my phobias, since my starvation days, was a fear of being without food. My common sense told me that it was a foolish fear, but phobias are not easy to dispel. An even greater phobia, although my common sense told me that I had no need to worry, was that someone would try to lift me by the fur at the back of my neck. This is such an evil practice that I am going to write a few lines about it. After all, if we cats do not tell people of our problems, then people will not know of them!

When I was about to have my third set of babies, Pierre, the French Gardener who was employed by Mme. Diplomat, suddenly picked me up by my neck fur. The pain on my neck muscles was very great indeed, and my babies just fell out of me and were killed on the stone pathway. The sudden shock harmed me internally. Mister the Veterinarian was summoned and he had to pack part of me with something to staunch the blood. "You have lost me five kittens! Pierre!" said Mme. Diplomat angrily. "I should deduct it from your wages."

"But Madame," whined Pierre, "I was most careful I lifted her by the scruff of her neck, she must be a sickly creature, there is ALWAYS something wrong with her."

Mister the Veterinarian was red faced with anger, "This cat is being ruined!" he shouted, "Adult cats should NEVER be lifted by their fur, only FOOLS would treat expensive animals so!" Mme. Diplomat was furious at the loss of money which the death of my children had caused, at the same time she was a little puzzled; "But Monsieur," she said, "Mother cats CARRY their kittens by the fur of their necks, what is wrong with that?" "Yes! Yes! Madame," replied Mister the Veterinarian, "but the Mother cat carries her children thus when they are only days old. When the kittens are DAYS old they are so light that no harm at all is caused. Adult cats should always be lifted so that the weight is taken by the chest and the back legs. Otherwise a cat may be harmed internally."

I am a silly Old Woman Cat, but I am afraid of being picked up by anyone except my Family. The Guv WON'T LET any stranger pick me up, anyway, so what am I worrying about? He picks me up better than anyone else, and this is how he does it - - the correct way. He puts his left hand under my chest, between my forelegs where they join the body. His right hand supports either the front of my thighs, or he allows me to stand with my back legs on his right hand.

When holding a nervous or strange cat, one should always have the right hand supporting the front of the thighs, then the cat cannot kick or leap away, and it is the most painless way of holding cats. People have said to the Guv, "Oh, I always pick them up by the back of the neck as some cat books say!" Well, no matter what "some cats books say," we, the cats, know what we prefer, and now YOU know too! So PLEASE, if you love us cats, if you want to spare us pain or injury, Lift us as described above. How would YOU like to be lifted by the back of YOUR neck, or by your hair? We HATE it!

Nor do we like to have silly "Puss Puss" talk. We understand ANY language if the person will think what he or she is saying. Baby talk irritates us and makes us wholly unco- operative. We have brains and know how to use them. One of the many things that amazes us about humans is that they are so sure we are merely "dumb animals", so sure that there is no other form of sentient life than humans, so sure that there CANNOT be life on other worlds, for humans believe most strongly that they are the highest form of evolution!

Let me tell you something; we do not speak English, nor French, nor Chinese, not so far as the sounds go, but we understand those languages. We converse by thought. We "understand" by thought. So did humans before . . . yes, before they were treacherous to the animal world and so LOST the power of thought reading! We do not use "reason" (as such) we have no frontal lobes; we KNOW by intuition. The answers "come" to us without us having to work out the problems. Humans use a telephone in order to speak over a distance. They have to know a "number". We cats when we know the "number" of the cat to whom we desire to speak, can send our messages over hundreds of miles by telepathy. Very rarely can humans understand our telepathic messages. Ma can sometimes. The Guv can always.

Well, as Miss Ku has just reminded me, this is a long way from writing about our first car in Canada. But I still say, with all respect to Miss Ku, that it is good to get a cat's opinion on the best way to lift and treat -- a cat.

On the following morning the mailman brought letters, heaps of letters. The Guv looked at the envelopes and I heard the sound of paper being slit. There was a rustling as the Guv drew a letter from its envelope, then silence for a moment while he read. "Oh!" he said, "these Canadians are savage!

Here is a letter from the Ministry of Health, telling me that if I do not report forthwith I am liable to be DEPORTED!"

Ma took the letter and read it herself. "First time they have written to you, wonder why they write in such a nasty way?" she said. "I don't know," replied the Guv, "all I know is that I bitterly regret coming to this awful country!" He went on to read other letters. "One here from Customs saying that our goods -- the things sent by sea -- have arrived and someone has to go to Customs about it. That's in Ouellette." "I'll go," said Ma, bustling off to get ready.

Just in time for lunch, Ma returned. "I don't know why these Canadian officials are so unpleasant," she said as she came in. "They tried to make trouble because of the type- writers. They said that if we wanted an electric typewriter it should have been bought in Canada. I told them it was bought BEFORE we even thought on coming to this country. It is all settled now, but they were very unpleasant!" She sat down and we had lunch.

"Who wants a ride?" asked the Guv. "ME!" yelled Miss Ku rushing to the door. "I'll stay home and keep Fifi company," said Ma. The Guv, Miss Ku, and Buttercup went out and I heard the garage door being opened and the car started. "There they go, Feef," said Ma, running her hand up and down my spine. "They are going to look round Windsor." We pottered around, I helped Ma make the beds, I would run up and down on the sheets and it would straighten them out fine. We had to deal with tradesmen at the door, the bread man and the milkman and someone who came to ask the name of the landlord. Cars were rushing about outside, I never could understand why everyone traveled around so.

An hour or so later the Guv drove back. Buttercup carried in Miss Ku so that her feet should not get cold on the snow. The Guv locked the garage and came in for tea. "Not like beautiful Dublin, Feef," said Miss Ku, "Windsor is a very small city, and all the men seem to smoke strong cigars and say 'waal I guess.' We went down a street and I thought there were big skyscrapers in the street. When we got to the bottom I saw a river and the big buildings were in Detroit."

"The man has brought our cases from the Customs," said Ma. Slowly the various cases were carried in. Cases of clothing, cases of books, a tape recorder, and the big electric typewriter. Throughout the rest of the afternoon we were busy unpacking. Miss Ku and I did our share by examining everything and by raking out clothes and paper. The Guv opened the great packing case containing the typewriter. "It saved a lot of time," he said, "having the motor changed to the Canadian voltage. Now we can start another book without delay." Stooping, he picked the machine off the floor and set it on a table. Inserting a sheet of paper, and plugging the cable into a power socket, he sat down to type. The machine spluttered and jerked. The Guv became crosser and crosser.

Getting up, he went to the electric meter board and read "115 volts 60 cycles." Going back to the typewriter and turning it upside down, he read "115 volts 50 cycles." "Rab!" he called, "they have fixed the wrong motor on this machine. It can't be used!" "Let's ring up the makers," said Ma, "they have a place in Windsor." WEEKS later we found that the makers were not interested nor would they make any allowance on a trade-in, nor would they sell the machine. At last the Guv just traded in the machine for an ordinary portable of a different maker, and through a different firm.

Buttercup uses that machine. The Guv uses the same old Olympia Portable on which he wrote "The Third Eye", "Doctor from Lhasa", "The Rampa Story", and is now typing my book for me.

One day Ma and Buttercup went into Windsor to buy some peat moss for Miss Ku and me. As soon as they returned Miss Ku said, darkly, "There is something in the wind, Feef, you mark my words! Buttercup is out of herself: There is something in the wind!" She nodded her head sagely and wandered off, muttering beneath her breath. "Sheelagh has seen a monkey!" said Ma. The Guv sighed, "Surely she has seen plenty of them before?" he said. "Hey, Feef!" whispered Miss Ku, rushing back to me, "THAT is why she smells so strange, she has been near a monkey. Holy Tomcats! One never knows what that young woman is going to do next!"

"How would you like to have a monkey in the house?" Ma asked the Guv. "Good Grief!" he retorted, "don't I live with you two now?" "No, seriously," said Ma, "Sheelagh wants a monkey!" "Buttercup, Buttercup, oh! Buttercup, what have you done now?" asked Miss Ku. "Feef!" she whispered "The Old Man's taken a blow over this, A MONKEY! What next will she want?"

The Guv was sitting on a chair, I went over to him and rubbed my head against his leg to show that I sympathized with him. He ruffled my fur and turned to Buttercup. "What is it all about, anyhow?" he asked her. "Well," she said, "we went in to get the peat moss and there was this monkey sitting mournfully on the bottom of a cage. He's SWEET! I asked the man to let me see him and it seems that he has cage paralysis from being confined too long. But he will soon recover if we have him," she added quickly. "Well, I can't stop you," said the Guv, "if you want a monkey, go and get it. They are messy things, though." "Oh! Do come and look at him," said Buttercup, excitedly. "He's SWEET!" Sighing so deeply that I heard his buttons creak, the Guv stood up.

"Come on, then," he said, "or we shall be in the evening rush of traffic." Buttercup raced around in a flurry of excitement, rushed up the stairs, and rushed down again. Miss Ku laughed to herself as they went out. "You should see the Guv's face!" she said.

That is one thing I WOULD like to do, see the Guv's face. I know he is bald, bearded, and big, Miss Ku describes people for me -- and does it well -- but there is nothing that can take the place of actually seeing. We blind people do develop a "sense" though, we form a sort of mental image of what a person looks like. We can feel a person's face, sniff them, and tell much from their hand-touch and from their voice. But a person's coloring, that is quite beyond us.

We wandered round, half our minds on the house, and the tea which was being prepared, and the other half on the Guv and Buttercup, wondering whatever they would bring back.

"I lived for several days in a monkey cage, Miss Ku," I said by way of making conversation. "Huh? Well, they should have kept you there, I guess!" said Miss Ku. "Monkeys? Who wants monkeys?" she went on in an aggrieved tone. We sat and waited. Ma had the tea ready and then she sat by us and probably thought of monkeys too! "I'm going upstairs to look out of the bathroom window," said Miss Ku, "I'll give you the wire as soon as I see anything," she added as she turned and ran lightly up the stairs. A boy came to the door bringing the evening paper. Ma went and fetched it from the rack and came in to scan the headlines. Not a sound from Miss Ku, ensconced in the bathroom window. We waited.

Chapter Eight

The door opened. The Guv and Buttercup entered. From the manner in which they were walking I knew they were carrying something heavy or bulky. Miss Ku rushed to my side. "Phew! What a pong!" she exclaimed. I wrinkled my nose, there WAS an acrid smell around, a smell like wet rabbit, bad drains, and old tomcat. "Well, you cats," said the Guv, "come and say hello to the monkey." He put some- thing on the ground, and at the strangeness of my impressions I felt a thrill run along my spine and my tail began to fluff.

"Careful Feef!" exhorted Miss Ku. "We have a rum looking fellow here! He is in a great big parrot cage. Oh Golly!" she exclaimed in dismay, "He has sprung a leak!"

"Do you think we can get that chain off him?" asked Buttercup, "I'm SURE he would be all right without it."

"Yes," said the Guv, "let us take him out of the cage first." He moved to the cage and I heard the noise as of a small door being opened. Suddenly, appallingly, pandemonium broke out. A noise which was a cross between ships sirens which I had heard at New York Harbor and the fog horn at the Bailey Lighthouse, Dublin. Miss Ku backed off in consternation. "GEE!" she exclaimed, "I wish I could make a commotion like that and get away with it. Move back, Feef, he has sprung another leak." I backed several feet, not turning my back on the creature, then leaned over to Miss Ku and asked, "Is the thing being killed?" "Killed? Good Grief, no! The creature is neurotic, it started all that racket before it was even touched. The Guv is taking off a whacking great chain so the thing will be more comfortable."

"Put some newspapers on the floor," said the Guv," "let us have some use from the Press!" I heard the rustle of papers and then the creature began to scream, whistle and hoot again. "Miss Ku," I asked, "How do we address the thing?"

"I'm going to call it Monkey rouse!" replied Miss Ku. "My Oh! My, Oh! My!" she added, "Buttercup has REALLY gone off her rocker now!" "Look Sheelagh," said the Guv, "If we hang the cage up here, between the two rooms, he will be able to see more, what do you think?" "Well, yes," she replied, "but I want him to be out of the cage." "Seems to me he needs attention," said the Guv, "Let us get a Vet here to look at him." "Feef!" whispered Miss Ku, "BEAT IT! A Vet is coming, he might get at our ears." To be on the safe side, we retreated to the shelter of the underside of the Guv's bed.

Ma came back from the telephone. "The Vet will be here tomorrow," she said, "he did not want to come, but as I told him, we could hardly bring a monkey to him. He will be here at about eleven in the morning." "Okay, Feef," said Miss Ku, "Saved by the gong, we can get out again." "Miss Ku," I said, "what does this monkey look like?"

"Look like? Oh! Like nothing on Earth! Ugly critter indeed. Last time saw anything so awful was when Buttercup had a baby last. That was in England, you know. The thing was a Tom and he had a face like this monkey, or the monkey has a face like that little Tom. Wrinkled, wizened, helpless. Makes strange meaningless sounds and is always leaking." Miss Ku paused reminiscently, "Ah! Those were strange days," she said, "Buttercup used to have a husband then one day she said 'YEOW! I'm going to have a baby!' and she did, there and then. Now she's got herself a monkey! Tsk! Tsk!"

"Hate, hate!" said Monkeyrouse, "Hate, hate, hate all. Shop life bad. Dint wanta go. Eddie sell me short. Hate!"

"Miss Ku," I said, in some consternation, "Do you think we should have a word with Monkeyrouse? We CANNOT have all that hate here, this is a GOOD household." "Aw! De guy is nuts!" replied Miss Ku, who sometimes relapsed into Canadian or American. "Nuts? Nuts?" said Monkeyrouse, "Catsisnuts! I good American, hate all others. Crazy cats keep away."

The Guv came over and picked me up in his arms. "Feef," he said, "I will hold you close to the cage and you tell the monkey he is being foolish. He cannot reach out and touch you, Feef." "Hate all! Hate all!" screeched Monkeyrouse, "Git outa here! Git outa here!" I felt intense sorrow that any creature would be so foolish, so misguided and so spiritually blind. "Monkeyrouse!" I said, "Listen to me, we want to make you happy, we want you to come out of that cage and play with us, we will look after you." "Crazy Old Woman Cat! Crazy Old Woman Cat!" screeched Monkeyrouse, "Git outa here." The Guv rubbed my chin and chest. "Never mind, Feef," he said, "perhaps he will come to his senses if we let him go a bit." "Okay, Guv," I replied, "Miss Ku and I will look after him and will tell you if we get through to him. I think he has been in a shop too long. He is neurotic. Still, time will tell."

"Hey, Guv." called Miss Ku, "let me have a word with Buttercup. If she put him on the floor, out of his cage, he may feel better."

The cage was suspended in the archway between two rooms. The Guv tried to lift Monkeyrouse out while Buttercup held the cage steady. The air was rent, no, SHREDDED, by the screams of Monkeyrouse who clung to the cage and shrieked and shrieked and shrieked. "Gor!" said Miss Ku, "this sure is a neurotic monkey." "Hate! HATE!" screamed Monkeyrouse. At last he was out and sitting upon the floor. I heard a trickling noise and started to move forward to investigate: "Mind!" said Miss Ku, "If you come forward you will have to jump the Yellow Sea. And if you don't look out," she roared, "you will be caught by the advancing waves."

"Rab!" "Yes?" replied Ma. "How about wrapping up the cats and taking them down to the edge of the water? Poor old Ku is killing herself to look out." Miss Ku and I have special jackets for cold weather, they are knitted of thick wool and have armholes and they keep us really warm. Now, with these on, and each of us wrapped in an even warmer rug, we were ready to be carried out. The Guv carried Miss Ku, be- cause he and Miss Ku were more adventurous. Ma carried me. We opened the door at the other side of the sun porch and stepped down to the snow covered grass. By the time which we were walking I estimated that the back garden was about three houses long. At the end there was a broad stone wall beyond which was the frozen lake. "Be careful," said the Guv to Ma and me, "It is very slippery here." "Ohhh!" screamed Miss Ku, "Isn't the lake BIG! Oh, Feef," she ex- claimed, turning to me, "It is like a sea, as big as the sea at Howth. And it is frozen. Now let me see, what can I tell you about it? Oh yes, I know, before me is the lake. To my left there is an island and on the tip of it there is a tower where men watch so that no one can steal the ice. They should buy refrigerators, you see, and make business," she added.

"Right in front, in the distance I can see America and to the right the lake swells out becoming bigger and bigger." "How are you doing, Feef?" asked the Guv, "not feeling cold?" I told him that I was doing fine and enjoying the change.

"Ku," said the Guv, "are you a brave Big Girl Cat?"

"Me? Of course I am!" replied Miss Ku. "All right, hold on tightly," said the Guv, "you and I will go down on to the ice then you can tell Feef all about it." Miss Ku squealed with delight. I heard the sound of climbing footsteps on frozen wood and Miss Ku called from the distance, "Hey, Feef, I'm being kept on ice. My! It is thick. I could walk to America, Feef!"

We were glad to get indoors, though, where it was warm, and where Buttercup was nursing Monkeyrouse -- whic showed quite a lot of faith. As we entered, she stood up quickly, and put the monkey on the floor. "Oh! BOTHER!" she said, "all over my clean dress." Miss Ku turned to me, "Tsk! Tsk!" she muttered, "remind ME never to have a * * * * * monkey, Feef!"

The storm raged all night. "Worst for years!" said the Wise Ones who brought the bread and the milk. "More coming," they said. We knew, too, for we also listened to the radio reports. Water pipes in the basement were frozen solid.

"A pity Monkeyrouse's water pipes don't freeze," said Miss Ku, gloomily. The Vet of Monkeys had been, and to our great delight, had gone. "No cure," he said, "Try massaging his legs, MIGHT help, but I doubt it, been left too long."

With a quick shake of his head he had gone. We came from under the Guv's bed. The roofing of the next house was banging. Somewhere a can was rolling along the snow covered road under the in- fluence of the wind. Monkeyrouse was sitting in the middle of the floor. We were sitting on a sofa. "WHOUF!" said the wind, taking a mighty breath. "BAM? RRRIPPP!" said our double window as it blew into the room, bringing the storm with it. Buttercup raced into the room, scooped up Monkeyrouse and fled to a distant bedroom with him. Miss Ku and I hurried underneath the Guv's bed to await developments. The Guv grabbed tools, nails and materials and hurried out into the storm, anxious to do something before the roof blew off or the walls blew in. Down the stairs clattered Buttercup, clad in raincoat and anything that would keep out wind and snow. "Creepin' Caterpillars!" muttered Miss Ku, "we poor cat people will be blown across the ice to America if they don't hurry up." The house was shaking to the fury of the gale. The Guv and Buttercup wrestled with sheets of plastic and lumps of wood. Wrestled, and nearly got blown away when the wind got under the plastic sheet. Ma tussled mightily to hold the curtains together so that the snow would not fill the room. Upstairs Monkeyrouse was shrieking like a mad thing. Around the house the wind was doing the same. At last the Guv and Buttercup came in, having patched up the broken window.

"Get on to the Landlord," said the Guv, "tell him we have made a temporary repair, but if he does not get it done properly the whole roof will go!" "The Guv is looking dreadful," said Miss Ku, "it is his heart, you know."

The winter seemed endless. Miss Ku and I thought Canada was somewhere near the North Pole. Day after day was the same, dull weather, falling snow and freezing temperatures. Miss Ku did a lot of motoring, attending to the shopping and telling the Guv where to drive. She would call to following drivers, admonishing them not to 'tail-gate' and reprimanding them for their bad driving habits. One day the Guv and Buttercup asked her to go to Detroit with them. Off they went, leaving Ma and me to do the housework. Monkeyrouse was in his cage. When they returned Miss Ku walked in with a jaunty air, her tail straight up.

"You may sit beside me, Feef," she said, graciously, "and I will tell you about Detroit. You need to have your mind broadened, anyhow." "Yes, Miss Ku," I replied, flattered that she should take so much trouble to tell me. I moved over to where she was impatiently tapping the ground with her tail, and sat down. She settled herself comfortably, and idly combed her vibrissal as she talked.

"Well, it is like this," she commenced, "we left this dump and drove along to where old Hiram makes his whiskey. That's near the place the Guv went to have his lungs tested. We turned left and went over the railroad tracks and then right into Wyandotte. We drove on until I thought we had gone far enough to arrive back in Ireland, then the Guv turned right and left again. Some guy in a uniform waved us on and we managed to get beneath the ground. I was not at all frightened, mind you, but we careered along a dimly-lit tunnel. The Guv told me that we were going under the Detroit River. I could well believe it, that is what it felt like, that is why I had chills up and down my spine. We drove on and up and turned where a sign said 'Slippery when wet' and then we paid some money. A few feet further on a man stuck his ugly head in the window and said "Whereyabawnfolks?"

The Guv told him, and Buttercup -- as usual -- said her piece, and the man said "O-kay" and we drove off.

"It must have been very wonderful, Miss Ku," I said, "I, would dearly love to be able to see such wonders." "Phooey!" said Miss Ku, "you ain't seen nuthin' yet. Get a load of this.

We drove out into a big street with buildings so high that I expected to see angels sitting on their tops -- on the tops of the buildings, of course, the angels would be sitting on THEIR bottoms. Cars were racing along as if the drivers had gone mad, but of course they were Americans. We drove on a bit and then I saw the water and two white ships moored with their winter overcoats on so as to keep the snow out. The Guv said that the canvas coverings would be taken off and the ships would take a lot of Americans somewhere and back.

For that they would pay money." I nodded, knowing something about such things, because I had been on a ship at Marseilles, far away on the shores of the warm Mediteranean. I smiled as I thought that now I was sitting looking after a mad monkey in frozen Canada. "Don't keep interrupting Feef," said Miss Ku. "But I did not say a word, Miss Ku!" I replied. "No, but you were thinking of other things; I want your undivided attention if I am to continue." "Yes, Miss Ku, I am all attention," I replied. She sighed and continued, "We looked in some whacking great shops. Buttercup had a yen for shoes. While she was looking down at shoes I lay upon my back so that I could look up at a bigger than big building. The Guv told me that that particular building was called 'Pin-up Scott' or something, but I did not find out why he was going to be pinned up. Well, at long last Buttercup decided she had seen enough of shoes, so they could give a little attention to Poor Old Ku once again.

We drove along a terrible road, so rough that I thought my teeth would drop out and the Guv said we were 'in Porter.' First I thought it was the porter one drinks (not me, of course) and then I thought it was a man who carried things. Eventually I saw it was Porter Street. We turned left and hit such a bump in the road that I thought the wheels had dropped off. The Guv handed some money to another guy in uniform and we went past a row of little huts where they controlled traffic. As I looked up I saw a structure like a giant Meccano thing and on it was labeled 'Ambassador Bridge'. We drove on and -- OW! -- the view! Coming into Detroit we had gone under the river, with the ships' bottoms above us. Now, going back to Canada we were so high that an American would say we were intoxicated.

"We stopped on the Bridge and looked out. Detroit spread before us like one of the models which I had seen the Guv make. Train ferries were carrying railroad cars across the water. A speedboat came racing along, and the great lake ships looked like toys in a bathtub. Wind struck the Bridge and it shook a little. So did I. 'Let's get outta here, Guv!' I said, and he said all right, so we drove on to the end of the Bridge. 'WhafFewgotfolks?' asked a man in uniform, giving me a scary look. 'Nothing,' said the Guv. So we drove on some more, all the way through Windsor and here we are!"

"My!" I breathed, "you HAVE had an adventure!" But it was as nothing to the adventure she was going to have in a few days' time.

The Guv is very particular about cars. Things have to be just right, and if a car is not as the Guv thinks it should be, it gets attention immediately. About three, or was it four? days after Miss Ku went on her trip to Detroit, the Guv came in and said, "I'm not satisfied with the car steering. There seems to be a tight bearing." Ma said, "Take it up the road to that Service Station, it will be quicker than going all the way to Windsor." The Guv went off. Soon after I thought I heard the sound of a Police siren, but passed over the vague idea. Half an hour or so later, a car drew up, a door slammed, and the Guv came into the house as the car drove off. "Done already?" asked Ma. "No!" said the Guv, "I came back in a taxi. Our car will not be ready until this afternoon, it needs new steering ends, but it will be all right when those are replaced." "What's happened?" asked Ma, who knows the Guv's expressions well. "I was doing about twenty- five miles an hour up the road," replied the Guv, "when a Police siren went off just behind me. A Police car shot ahead and pulled up directly in front of me. I stopped, of course, and a Police- man got out of his car and came lumbering towards me. I wondered what I had done wrong -- I had been driving five miles under the limit. 'You Lobsang Rampa?' the Policeman asked. 'Yes,' I replied, 'I read one of your books' said the man. Anyhow," said the Guv, "He only wanted to talk and he told me that Press Reporters were still trying to trace us."

"Pity they haven't got something better to do," said Ma.

"We don't want anything to do with the Press, they have told lies enough about us."

"What time is it?" asked the Guv. "Three thirty," replied Ma. "I think I will go and see if the car is ready. If it is I will come back and collect you and Miss Ku and we will go out and try it." Ma said, "Shall I telephone them? If they will deliver the car -- if it is ready -- you can drive the mechanic back to the garage and then come for us. I'll phone now," said Ma, hurrying off to the foot of the stairs where we kept the telephone. Miss Ku said, "Oh! Goody; I'm going out, Feef, is there anything you want?" "No thank you, Miss Ku," I replied, "I hope you will have a pleasant trip." Ma came hurrying back; "The mechanic is on his way now," she said. "By the time you get on your coat he should be here."

The Guv did not wear a thick overcoat, like other people, he just wore something light in order to keep the snow off. It often made me smile when the Guv was out in just trousers and jacket while everyone else was SWADDLED with everything they could cram on!

"The car is at the door," called Buttercup from upstairs where she was entertaining Monkeyrouse. "Thank you!" replied the Guv as he went out to where the mechanic was waiting in the big green Monarch car. "Come on, Miss Ku, said Ma, "we have to be ready, he will not be more than a few minutes." Miss Ku tripped daintily along so that Ma could help her with her coat, the blue woolen one with the red and white edging. The car was heated, but the path to the car was not. "I'll think of you, Stick-in-themud!" said Miss Ku to me, "while I am bowling along the highway you will be listening to the shrieks of Monkeyrouse." "He's come," said Ma. "Goodbye Miss Ku," I called, "look after yourself."

The doors shut, the car drove off, and I sat down to wait. It was terrible to be alone; I depended utterly upon the Guv and Miss Ku, they were my eyes, and often my ears. As one gets older, particularly after a very hard life, one's hearing becomes less acute. Miss Ku was young, and always had had the best food. She was vital, healthy, and alert and with a brilliant intellect. I -- well, I was just an old woman cat wh had had too many kittens, too many hardships.

"They are a long time, Feef!" said Buttercup, coming down the stairs after settling Monkeyrouse. "They are indeed!" I replied before I remembered that she did not understand the Cat language. She went to the window and looked out, then busied herself with food. As far as I remember now, it was something to do with fruit and vegetables, for Buttercup was VERY fond of fruit. Personally I disliked fruit intensely, except for coarse grass. Miss Ku was fond of a grape now and then, the white ones, she liked to have them skinned and then she would sit and suck them.

Curiously enough, she (Miss Ku) also liked roast chestnuts. I once knew a cat, in France, who ate prunes and dates!

Buttercup switched on the lights, "It is getting late, Feef, I wonder what is keeping them?" she said. Outside, the traffic was roaring along the road as people from Windsor returned home after their day in the shop or office or factory. Other cars raced in the opposite direction as people on pleasure bent (they would be 'broke' after!) went in search of amusement across the River. Cars -- cars -- cars everywhere, but not the one I wanted to see.

Long after the last homing bird had shaken the snow from her night- perch and tucked her head beneath her wing in sleep, there came at last the slam of a car door. In came the Guv, and Ma, and Miss Ku. "What happened?" asked Buttercup. "What happened?" I echoed. Miss Ku rushed to me breathlessly, "Come under the bed, Feef, I must tell you!" Together we turned and went into the Guv's bed- room and under the bed where we had our conferences. Miss Ku settled herself and folded her arms. From the room outside came a murmur of voices. "Well, Feef, it was like this," said Miss Ku. "We got in the car and I said to the Guv 'let's wring this thing out' I said, 'let's see how it goes.' We went up the road and on through Tecumseh -- that's the place I told you about before where they nearly all speak French -- and then we turned on to one of the superhighways where you put your foot on the gas pedal and forget all about it." Miss Ku paused a moment, to see that her tale was having the right effect on me. Satisfied that I was paying sufficient attention, she continued, "We beetled along somewhat for a time and then I said, 'Gee, Guv, press the jolly old gas pedal down, what?' He speeded the contraption up a bit but I saw that we were only doing sixty, which was very legal. We went some more, maybe sixty five, then there was a clang and a shower of sparks (like Guy Fawkes Night) shot out beneath us and trailed astern. I looked at the Guv and then hastily looked away. The wheel was loose in his hand!" She paused again in order to build up the suspense and when she ob- served that I was fairly panting, she resumed.

"There we were, on the long long highway, doing sixty five and a lick more. We had no steering, the track rods had dropped off. Fortunately there was not much traffic. The Guv managed somehow to pull up the car and it slithered to a halt with one front wheel hanging over a ditch. The air was full of the smell of burning rubber because he had had to put on the brakes hard in order to keep us from turning over in the ditch. The Guv got out, turned the front wheels by hand, and then got back and used reverse gear to get us on the road again. Ma got out and walked to a place where they had a telephone and called the garage to come and pick up the pieces. Then we all sat in the car together while we waited for the breakdown truck to come for us."

I marveled, Miss Ku showed no signs of strain, she was calm and collected. I could hardly wait for her to continue.

"But Miss Ku," I prompted her, "the steering had just been repaired -- that is why the car was at the garage!" "Sure, Bud, sure," replied Miss Ku, "all the steering things that had been replaced dropped off because the split pins or some- thing had been forgotten. Well, as I was saying, a breakdown truck with a great crane on the back of it came miles to meet us. The man got out and made 'tsk! tsk! and you are still alive?' noises. We all manhandled the car so that the truck could get in front. I sat on the front seat and yelled over the noise telling everyone what to do. Oh! It was a real do, Feef" she exclaimed, "I haven't told you the half of it.

Well, the three of us got in the front seat of the Monarch, and the crane lifted the front wheels clear of the ground. I thought how undignified we must look, then the truck started on the way home, with us swaying and jolting behind. We did miles, and I say to this day that the fast tow back damaged our automatic transmission." She snorted dourly at me and said, "You are not an engineer, Feef, if you were you would know that it is very damaging to tow a car with automatic transmission. Too fast a tow can wreck everything, and this tow did. But there, I am not giving a technical lecture, it would be beyond you anyhow, Feef."

"Miss Ku," I asked, "what happened then?" "Happened then? Oh, yes, we rattled over the railroad crossing at Tecumseh and soon were in front of the garage. The Guv was cross because he had paid to have all those parts replaced, but the garage man would not admit liability, saying it was 'an act of God,' whatever that means. He had us driven home in his own car, though, because I told him I could not carry the Guv all that way. So here we are!" I could hear the rattle of dishes, and thought it was time to see about some food for us, I had not been able to eat while waiting and worrying.

First I had one question; "Miss Ku, were you not frightened?" I asked. "Frightened? FRIGHTENED? Glory Be and Ten Tomcats, no. I knew that if anyone could get us out of the mess the Guv could, and I was there to advise him. Ma kept very calm, we did not have any trouble with her. I thought perhaps she might panic and scratch, but she took it all as a matter of course. Now for the eats!" We rose from our seats beneath the bed and wandered out into the kitchen where supper was ready.

"Old Man's holding forth," said Miss Ku, "wonder what's biting him now?" We hurried up with our supper so that we could go in and listen without losing too much food or knowledge. "Get a move on, Feef'" urged Miss Ku, "we can wash while we listen." We moved into the living room and sat down to wash after our supper and pick up all the news.

"I'm tired of that car!" grumbled the Guv, "we should change it for something better." Ma made noises, clearing her throat and all that, which indicated she was dubious.

"Hark at Ma!" whispered Miss Ku, "she is counting out the shekels!" "Why not wait?" asked Ma, "we are still waiting for those royalties, they should be here any day now."

"WAIT?" asked the Guv, "if we change cars now we still have something with which to do an exchange. If we wait until we can afford it, the old Monarch will have fallen to pieces and be worthless. No! If we wait until we can AFFORD to do it, we shall never do it." "Monkeyrouse has been terrible," said Buttercup, changing the subject, "I don't know what we can do with him." Miss Ku told her, and it was fortunate that Buttercup did not understand the Cat language. The Guv did, and applauded, giving Butter- cup a polite and highly censored translation!

That night as I lay down to sleep I thought how dangerous these cars were. Pay a lot to have them serviced, and then bits dropped off and made more costs. It seemed fantastic to me that people wanted to go careering round the countryside in a tin box on wheels. Dangerous in the extreme I called it, much preferring to stay at home and never move out again.

I had done too much traveling, I thought, and where had it got me? Then I awakened with a jolt; it had got me to Ireland and if I had not moved to that country I should not have been able to meet the Guv, Ma, Buttercup, and Miss Ku. Now fully awake, I sauntered out into the kitchen to get a light meal in order to while away some of the night hours.

There I met Miss Ku who had been unable to sleep for thinking over the dangerous hours of the day. Monkeyrouse chattered irritably and -- as always with Monkeyrouse -- I heard water splashing. Miss Ku nudged my elbow and muttered, "Bet the Detroit River has been much deeper since that thing came to live with us. Buttercup must have gone off her head to want such a creature!" "Hate! Hate" screamed Monkeyrouse into the night air. "Goodnight, Feef," said Miss Ku. "Goodnight, Miss Ku," I replied.

The next morning the Guv went up to the garage to see what could be done about the car. He was away most of the morning and when he came back he was driving the Mon- arch. The Guv always has a Family Conference when there is anything important to be decided. That is an Eastern trait to which we cats subscribe, Miss Ku and I always discussed things before one of us did anything important. At the Family Conference the Guv and I sat together, and Ma and Miss Ku sat together. Buttercup sat alone because Monkeyrouse had no intellect and merely shrieked "Hate! HATE! Wanna leave! Dint wanta come!" "First," said the Guv, "we shall have to move out of this house. I understand from the garage people that the other side of the road is going to be used as a city garbage dump, they are going to fill in the ditch with refuse. That will bring hordes of flies in the summer. Then this road is almost impassable in the summer because of the American trippers. So -- we are going to leave."

He stopped and looked round. No one moved, no one said a word. "Next," he continued, "the steering has been put in order on this car, but it will soon want a lot of money spent on it. I consider that we should go to Windsor and trade in this car for another. The third thing is, what are we going to do about Monkeyrouse? He is becoming worse, and as the Vet says, he will need more and more attention. Shall we let that man have him? He knows all about monkeys." For quite a time we sat and discussed things. Cars, houses, and monkeys. Miss Ku made notes of every thing, she had a very good head for business and could always deal with other peoples'.

"I think we should go into Windsor this morning," said Ma, "if you have it on your mind it is just as well to get it over. I want to look at a house as well." "Golly!" muttered Miss Ku, "action at last! They sure are hot stuff this morning."

"Well, Sheelagh, what about Monkeyrouse?" asked the Guv of Buttercup. "We had him to see if he could be cured," she replied, "and as he obviously is getting no better, and is missing the other animals, I think he should go back."

"Right," answered the Guv, "we will see what can be done. We are going to have a full week." Miss Ku interrupted to say how foolish it was, living out in the wilds away from Windsor. "I want to see the shops, to see LIFE!" she said.

"We will find a place right in Windsor this time," said the Guv. Ma got up, "We shan't find anywhere if we just sit here," she said, "I will go and get ready." Off she hurried, and the Guv went out to say rude things to the Monarch which had let us down.

Before Ma could get ready and go out to the car, the Guv returned. "That man up the road," he said, "he was passing by and saw me in the garage. He stopped to tell me that some Pressmen have been snooping around the place, trying to find out just where we live." The Family have been plagued by the Press, people came from many different parts of the world, all demanding an 'exclusive scoop.' We also got letters from all over the world and although not one in a thousand enclosed return postage the Guv replied to them all. He is becoming wiser, though, and no longer replies to ALL the letters. Miss Ku and I had to speak very strongly to him before he would use stern discrimination. That is one thing about him, he can be persuaded if one can show him the sense of a thing. Miss Ku and I often have to dig out facts in order to convince him, common sense is much more reliable than emotion.

The Guv called up the stairs to Buttercup, "Sheelagh! There are a crowd of Press dopes about. I suggest you don't answer the door, and make sure it is locked!" He and Ma went out, leaving Miss Ku and me to protect Buttercup from the Press. I heard the car start up, and the sounds as the Guv reversed it and turned. "Well, Old Woman Cat," said Miss Ku jovially, "I shall soon be driving in another and better car. YOU should try more motoring, Feef, it would broaden your outlook." "Mind yourselves, you cats," said Buttercup, coming down the stairs, "I want to do this floor." Miss Ku and I wandered off and sat on the Guv's bed. Miss Ku looked out of the window and told me of the scene. "The ice is breaking up on the Lake, Feef," she told me with glee. "I can see great chunks swirling away where the current is strong. That means the weather will soon be warmer. We might even be able to go in a boat, you'd like that, all the drink around you, you would never be thirsty."

We Siamese Cats are very gregarious, we MUST have LOVED people around us. Time dragged and almost stopped while we sat and waited. Buttercup was busy in the kitchen and we did not want to disturb her. Monkeyrouse was chanting away to himself "wantago wantago wantago. Hate all! Hate all!" I thought how tragic it was, here he had the best of homes and yet he was not satisfied! The French Carriage Clock struck eleven. I yawned and decided to have a nap in order to pass the time. Miss Ku was already asleep, her breath a gentle sound in the silence of the room.

Chapter Nine

"Gee! Oh Gee!" exclaimed Miss Ku with elan, "what a mighty fine automobile." Her voice rose higher and higher as she fairly shrieked, "AND IT'S MY NEW CAR, it is stopping here!" She pressed her nose harder and harder against the glass of the kitchen window. "Great Tomcats!" she breathed, "a hard top, its blue, Feef, the color of your eyes, and it has a white top. Man! Is the Guv ever clever to get a heap like that!" "I must possess my soul in patience," I thought, "and wait until she tells me more." It is quite hard, at times, being blind and having to depend so much upon the good offices of others. A car the color of my eyes she had said. I was VERY flattered at that. With a white top, too.

That would make it very smart and show off the blue to the best advantage. But now I heard the car doors being shut, the Guv and Ma would be in soon: Footsteps coming nearer along the path. The opening of the screen door and the slam as the spring shut it after. Then they came in, the Guv and Ma. Buttercup came racing down the stairs, as eager as Miss Ku and

I. "Coming out to see it?" the Guv asked Miss Ku and me. I said "No, thank you very much, Miss Ku will describe it for me when she returns." The Guv and Buttercup, the latter carrying a well wrapped Miss Ku, went out to the car. I could pick up Miss Ku's telepathic thoughts as she wanted me to. "Scrumptious, Feef, beautiful smell of leather. Mats you can REALLY get your claws into. Great Jumping Grass- hoppers, there's ACRES of glass and room to sit just inside the rear window. We are just going for a breeze up the road, ta ta, Feef, see you later."

Some people say, "Well, Mrs. Greywhiskers, why could you not pick up the telepathic messages all the time?" The answer to that very sensible question is: if all cats used their telepathic powers at full strength constantly, the 'air' would be so full of noise that no one would understand any message.

Even humans have to regulate their radio stations in order to prevent interference. Cats get on the wavelength of the cat they desire to call and then distance does not matter, but any other cat listening on that wave length also hears the message, so privacy is lost. We use close-range speech when we want to converse privately, and use telepathy for long range discussions and messages and for broadcasting to the cat community. By knowing a cat's wavelength, determined from the basic frequency of the aura, one can converse with a cat anywhere, and language is no bar. Is NO ba r? Well, not much of a bar. People, and that includes cats, tend to think in their own language and to project thought-pictures directly constructed from their own culture and conception of things. I make no apology for going into some details on this, for if my book gives humans even a slight understanding of cat problems and thoughts it will be well worthwhile.

A human and a cat see the same thing, but from a different viewpoint. A human sees a table and whatever is on that table. A cat sees only the underside of the table. We see upwards, from the ground up. The underside of chairs, the view beneath a motor car, legs stretching upwards like trees in a forest. For us a floor is a vast plain dotted with immense objects and clumsy feet. A cat, no matter where he may be, sees the same type of view, and so another cat will make out the sense of a message. Picking up from humans is a different matter, for they project a picture the perspective, or view- point, of which is so utterly alien to us that we are sometimes puzzled. Cats live with a race of giants. Humans live with a race of dwarfs. Lie on the floor, with your head resting on the floor and then you will see as a cat sees. Cats climb on furniture, and on walls so that they may see as humans see and so understand the thoughts which come to them.

Human thoughts are uncontrolled and radiate everywhere. Only people like my Guv can control the radiation and spread of their thoughts so as not to 'jam' all others. The Guv told Miss Ku and me that humans conversed by telepathy many many years ago, but they abused the power badly and so lost it. This, the Guv says, is the meaning of the Tower of Babel. Like us, humans formerly used vocal speech for private talk within a group, and telepathy for long distance and group use. Now, of course, humans, or most of them, use vocal speech only.

Humans should never under-rate cats. We have intelligence, brains, and abilities. We do not use reason in the generally accepted sense of that word, we use 'intuition'. Things 'come to us,' we KNOW the answer without the necessity of having to work it out. Many humans will not believe this, but, as the Guv has just remarked, "If people, human people, would explore the things of THIS world before attempting Space they would be better fitted for the latter. And if it were not for the things of the mind there would be NO mechanical things at all, it takes a mind to think out a mechanical device."

Some of our legends tell of great things between humans and cats in the days of long ago before humans lost their powers of telepathy and clairvoyance. DID some human laugh at the idea of cats having legends? Then why not laugh at the human gypsies who have legends going back centuries?

Cats do not write, we do not need to, for we have total recall at all times, and can use the Akashic Record. Many human gypsies do not write either, but the stories they know are passed down through the centuries. Who understands cats? Do YOU? CAN you say that cats have no intelligence? Really you live with a race of people whom you do not know because we, the cat people, do not WANT to be known. I am hoping that some day the Guv and I may together write a book of cat legends, and it will be a book that will truly amaze humans! But all this is far removed from what I am writing about now.

The sun was shining warmly upon me through the kitchen window when Miss Ku returned. "Brrr!" she said as she came in, "It is cold out, Feef, good thing the car has such an efficient heater!" She went off in order to have some light refreshment after the excitement of the new car. I thought I would eat as well, knowing that she would like to have company. "Food tastes good, Feef," she said, "I guess the outing has perked up my appetite. You ought to take a ride, then maybe you will eat even more than you do now - if possible!"

I smiled with her, for I never disguised the fact that I liked my food. After years of semi-starvation it was nice and comforting to be able to eat just when one wanted to. As we sat together washing after our meal, I said, "Will you tell me about the car, Miss Ku, please?" She thought a moment as she washed behind her ears and combed her vibrissa. "I've told you about the color," she said, "and I suppose you want to know what happened. Well, we got in the car and the Guv told Buttercup and me all about it. The Guv and Ma drove to the car lot and there they examined a lot of cars.

The Manager knows the Guv well, and he pointed out this one as being very good. The Guv tried it, liked it, and bought it. The old Monarch was traded in. The Guv is going to take both of us out for a ride later, he is going to go specially slow for you."

Monkeyrouse was shrieking his head off again. "Wantago! Wantago!" he howled. Buttercup scolded him, but very kindly, for making such a noise. Monkeyrouse was insane, of that we were sure. Always complaints from him. "When are we going to take him back?" Buttercup asked the Guv.

"Hooray!" yelled Miss Ku, leaping into the air with joy, "Old Misery Monk is going, everything will be drier then! I wish HE would get his taps frozen!" The night before had been colder than usual, and we had had the water supply frozen. As Miss Ku so often remarked, Monkeyrouse was the wettest monkey ever.

"We should telephone and say we are taking him back," said the Guv, "can't just drop this creature on an unsuspecting world!" Ma went to the bottom of the stairs to phone. The Guv NEVER used a telephone if he could help it, because he often picked up the thoughts of a person instead of what they were saying -- two very different things! After a few incidents where the Guv had picked the wrong meaning, they made a rule that Ma or Buttercup should use the instrument. Ma acted as "business manager" because the Guv said she was more fitted to do it. Ma saw to all the accounts, but only because the Guv wanted it that way.

"Yes, it will be all right to take him back," said Ma, adding glumly, "but they will not refund any money!"

"Well, Sheelagh, what shall we do?" asked the Guv. Buttercup was so upset that she stammered a little and shuffled her feet. "Well," she said, "he is becoming no better and he obviously does not like it here. I think maybe he is afraid of the cats, or would be better in a house without cats. Let's take him back!" "SURE? QUITE sure?" pressed the Guv.

"Yes, we will take him back for his own good." "All right, I will get out the car now." The Guv got up and went out to the Garage. "Hate! Hate!" shrieked Monkeyrouse, "Wanta- go! Wantago!" Sadly Buttercup took him out of his cage and wrapped a blanket round him. The Guv came in and carried out the big cage and put it in the commodious car trunk. He sat in the car for a time, running the engine so that the heater could warm the car for Monkeyrouse. Then, satisfied with the temperature, he gave a toot on the horn for Buttercup. I heard the car door close and the sound of the engine speeding up and fading away into the distance.

The car was a beautiful one, and Miss Ku loved it dearly. I went out a few times, but as I have already said, I am not at all fond of cars. Once the Guv took Ma, Miss Ku and me to a pleasant place beneath the Ambassador Bridge. We sat in the car and the Guv opened the window a trifle so that I could catch the scent of Detroit across the River. Miss Ku reminds me that 'scent' is definitely the wrong word here, but it is at least a polite word! As we sat there, in the warmth of the car, Miss Ku described the scene for me; "Above us the Ambassador Bridge stretches across the Detroit River like a Meccano toy across a bathtub. Trucks -- that is American for lorries, Feef-- rumble across in an endless procession. Private cars there are in plenty. Sightseers stop their cars on the Bridge in order to take photographs. Across from us is a railroad marshalling yard, while to the right the Americans are building some big Hall because Americans like to go to such places and talk. Conferences, or Conventions, they call them, it really means that they get away from the Missus, freeload on drinks, and get tangled up with paid girl friends."

Miss Ku stopped a moment and then said, "My! How the ice is coming down! If we could catch some of it and save it until the summer we would make a fortune. Well, as I was saying, if you like I will get the Guv to take us over to Detroit." "No Miss Ku, no thank you," I replied nervously, "I fear that should not enjoy it a bit. As I cannot see there would be no point in me going. I'm sure the Guv would love to take you, though!" "You really are a drippish sissy, Feef!" said Miss Ku, "I'm ashamed at your stick-in-the-mudishness."

"Let's take the cats home and go house-hunting," said Ma.

"All right," replied the Guv, "time we moved, anyway, I didn't like that place from the start." I called out "Goodbye, Mister the Ambassador Bridge." I had previous associations with ambassadors and consuls and so I did not want to be at all disrespectful to that Bridge. The engine hummed into life, and Miss Ku called to the Guv, "O-KAY! Let 'er roll!" The Guv put a gentle pressure on a pedal and the car eased slowly up the snow covered slope and on to Riverside Drive. As we passed Windsor

Station a train hooted with impatience and I almost jumped out of my skin with fright. On we went, along by the side of the River, past the Drink Factory and on. We went by a Convent and Miss Ku made the remark that she always thought of Mr. Loftus, away in Ireland, when she passed the place. Mr. Loftus has a Daughter who is a Sister in a Convent, and we hear that she is doing very well indeed.

We pulled into the side of the road, after our long drive, and the Guv said, "Home, Feef, you will soon be having your tea. Shall we have tea first, Rab?" he asked, turning to Ma.

"Just as well," she said, "then we need not worry about the time." The Guv has had so much suffering that he has to eat often and little. Because of 'the lean years' before I came Home as the Old Apple Tree had predicted, I too had had hardship, and I too eat often and little. We went into the house, being carried by the Guv and Ma and well wrapped, for the snow was yet upon the ground. In the house Buttercup had tea ready, so I went to her and told her I was glad to be back.

Tea was soon over. The Guv stood up and said, "Well, let's be going or we shall be caught in the evening rush." He bade Miss Ku and me goodbye and told us to look after Buttercup. Then he went out, followed by Ma. Once again we heard the voice of the car engine dying away in the distance. Knowing that we should be left to our own resources for an hour or two, we first took some exercise, I chased Miss Ku around the room, then she chased me. Then we had a competition to see who could make the most holes in the newspaper in the shortest time. This soon palled, and anyhow we had no more newspaper. "Let's see who can walk on the stair rail farthest, Feef, without falling off!" suggested Miss Ku immediately followed by, "Oh! I forgot, you can't see, well, that's out." She sat down and gently scratched her left ear in the hope of obtaining a flash of inspiration.

"Feef!" she called. "Yes, Miss Ku?" I answered. "Feef, you tell me a story, one of the old legends will do. Talk softly, because I want you to lull me to sleep. You can go to sleep after," she added magnanimously. "Very good, Miss Ku," I replied, "I will tell you of the Cats who saved the Kingdom." "Gee! That's a dilly, well, get crackin' ." She settled herself comfortably, and I turned so that I would be facing her, and commenced.

"In the days of Long Ago, it might have been a thousand or a million years, the Island lay green and beautiful beneath the warm gaze of a gently smiling sun. The blue waters lapped playfully at the indolent rocks and sent showers of white spray into the air in which rainbows stretched all embracing arms. The land was fertile and luxuriant, with the tall, graceful trees reaching high into the heavens there to be caressed by balmy breezes. From the higher grounds rivers came bounding over huge boulders, to fall tinkling into great pools before spreading out and flowing more sedately into the ever welcoming sea. In the hinterland mountains rose and hid their crowns above the clouds, providing maybe foundations for the Homes of the Gods.

"Along the stretches of golden sands, fringed by the white foam of incoming waves, happy natives played, swam, and made love. Here there was nothing but peace, joy, and ineffable contentment. Here there was no thought for the future, no thought of sorrows or evil, but only joy beneath the gently waving palms.

"A broad road led inwards from the shore, disappearing into the cool dusk of an immense forest, to reappear miles away where the scene was very different. Here were temples, wrought in colored stone and metals such as silver and gold. Mighty spires which reached aloft to probe the skies, domed cupolas, and vast expanses of time-mellowed buildings. From a high temple embrasure came the notes of a deep-toned gong, scattering into flight thousands of birds who had been dozing in the sunlight along the hallowed walls.

"As the deep chimmng continued, yellow robed men hastened to a central building. For a time the rush continued, then it slackened and in the open all was quiet again. In the main Assembly of the immense Temple the monks shuffled uneasily, speculating upon the reason for the sudden call. At last a door clicked in the far recesses of the Temple and a small file of yellow robed men came into view. The obvious Leader, an old old man wizened and dried by the years, walked slowly ahead, escorted by two immense cats, cats with black tails, ears and mask, and white bodies. There was, it was clear, complete telepathic understanding between the old man and the cats. Together they walked to a podium, where the old man stood a moment, gazing out upon the sea of faces confronting him." 'Brothers of all degree' he said at last, slowly, 'I have called you here to tell you that this our Island is in mortal danger. For long we have suffered under the threat of the scientists who inhabit the land at the other side of the mountain. Cut off from us by a deep gorge which almost divides this Island, they are not easy of access. Within their territory science has supplanted religion; they have no God, no conception of the rights of others. Now, Brothers of all degree,' the old priest stopped, and looked sadly around. Satisfied that he had the rapt attention of his audience, he resumed, 'We have been threatened. Unless we bow the knee to the ungodly and become utterly subservient to these evil men, they threaten to destroy us with strange and deadly germs.'

He paused wearily, with the weight of his years heavy upon him. 'We, Brothers, are here to discuss how we may circumvent this threat to our existence and freedom. We know where the germ cultures are stored, for some of us have tried in vain to steal them that they may be destroyed. Yet we have failed and those whom we sent have been tortured and killed.'" 'Holy Father!' said a young monk, 'would these germ cultures be bulky, heavy to carry? Could a man steal them and RUN with them?' He sat down, overcome with his temerity in addressing the Holy Father. The Old Man looked sadly before him; 'Bulk?' he queried, 'there is no bulk. The germ cultures are contained within a tube which may be held between a finger and thumb, yet one drop would spread across our land and annihilate us. There is no bulk, but the germ culture is contained within a tower which is heavily guarded.' He paused again, and mopped his brow. 'To show their contempt of us they placed it at an open window, well within sight of all those whom we have sent into their land. A slender tree stretches a delicate branch across the window, a branch but as thick as my wrist. To show they have no fear of us they sent a message saying that we should pray until we were light headed and then perhaps the branch would support us.'

"The meeting continued into the early hours of the morning, monk discussing with monk ways and means of saving their people from destruction. 'Could we but knock it down so that it would break, they would be vanquished and we would be saved from destruction,' said one monk. 'That is so' said another, 'but if we could knock it down we could reach it, and if we could hold it we then would hold the power, for it is said that there is no antidote, no way of staving off the evil germs.'

"In an inner sanctum the old old man lay in exhaustion upon his couch. Beside him, guarding him, lay the two cats. 'Your Holiness,' said one by telepathy, 'could not I go into the land, climb the tree and remove the phial?' The other cat looked across at his companion, 'We will go together;' he said, 'it will double the chance of success.' The old priest pondered, thinking of all that was at stake. At last he spoke telepathically, 'You may have the solution,' he said, 'for no one but a cat could climb that tree and move out upon the branch. You may have the solution.' He lapsed into his private thoughts for a while, and no telepathic cat would ever intrude upon one's private thoughts. 'Yes, it may be the answer!' the old man said again. 'We will have you both carried up to and across the gorge that you be not tired and we will there await your safe return' He paused and then added, 'And we will tell no other what it is that we will do for even in a community such as this there are those who talk too freely.

Yes,!' he clapped his hands in delight, 'we will send an emissary to obtain their terms and that will distract their attention from you.'

"The days that followed were busy ones. The High Priest let it be known that he desired to send an Emissary, and an answer was received that it would be permitted. Men guarding the Emissary, and carrying two baskets, climbed the mountain passes to the gorge, crossed, and were in enemy territory. The Emissary went on into the enemy stronghold, and under cover of darkness the cats were released from the baskets. As silent as the night itself they made off. Stealthily they approached the tree and paused at its foot. Thoroughly they used their telepathic powers in order to determine the presence of any enemy. Cautiously one ascended, while the other used every telepathic ability in order to keep the closest watch: With infinite caution the climbing cat crawled along the branch until at last he could snatch the phial under the nose of the startled guard. Long before men could come pouring out of the tower, the two cats had dissolved into the darkness, carrying back to the old priest the phial which would safeguard his land for years to come. Now, in that land, Cats are Sacred to the country's descendants, and only the cat knows why!"

A gentle snore punctuated my closing sentence. I looked up and listened to make sure. Yes, it was a snore, a loud one this time. I smiled contentedly and thought, "Well, so I am a dull Old Woman Cat, but at least I can soothe Miss Ku to sleep!" She did not sleep long, however. Soon she sat up, tall and erect. "Start washing, Feef," she commanded, "they are on their way home and I cannot have you looking slovenly." Moments later we heard a car engine, followed by the rattle of the garage door. Then -- footsteps upon the path, and the Guv and Ma came in.

"How did you get on?" asked Buttercup, taking off her apron and putting it aside. "We have a place," replied the Guv, "suit us fine. I'll take you to see it if you like, we will take 'Fanny Flap' as well." The Guv often called Miss Ku 'Fanny Flap' because of the way she rushed round in her excitement. I was glad he did not ask me to go to the new Apartment, but the Guv knew that I hated such things, much preferring to wait until we ALL moved in together.

What was there for a blind cat? Why should I go when I knew nothing of the place, did not even know of objects to avoid? I preferred to wait until all was settled, all the furniture was in place, because then the Guv and Miss Ku would take me to each room and point out the location of things, and the Guv would lift me up and down to objects so that I could memorize how far I should have to jump. When I knew a place I could jump on to or off a chair and not miss or hurt myself I stand up and feel a rhair first so that I can avoid jumping into the back, then I jump up to wherever I want to be. Of course at times I bump into things, but I have wits enough not to bump into the same thing twice!

They were not away long. Upon their return Miss Ku came bustling over to me, "Get your ears back, Feef," she commanded, "it is time you were briefed. Now, the place is a house made into two apartments. We have taken the whole house so that the Guv can write another book. We shall live in the upstairs apartment. It has large rooms and looks over the Detroit River. There is a large railed balcony which the Guv says we can use when the weather is warmer. And Feef, there is an ATTIC where we can play and get ourselves covered with dust. You'll LOVE it!" So the Guv was going to do another book, eh? I knew that People had been impressing him with the need for another book, I knew that he had had some special instructions from discarnate entities.

Already the title had been decided upon. Miss Ku got my thoughts, "Yes!" she exclaimed gleefully, "As soon as we move in next week we are going to see Mrs. Durr and get some paper and so start the book." "Mrs. Durr?" I enquired, "who is Mrs. Durr?" "You don't know Mrs. Durr? Why EVERYONE knows her, she is a lady bookseller who for the moment is working for a Windsor firm, but she is soon to set up her own business. Don't know Mrs. Durr! Well well! Is that ever out of this world," she shook her head and muttered with disgust. "But what does she look like, Miss Ku?" I asked, "I cannot see, you know!" "Oh no, of course, I forgot that," said Miss Ku, greatly mollified. "Sit ye down, Old Woman Cat, and I'll tell you." We climbed up to the windowledge and sat facing each other. Miss Ku said, "Well, you have missed something. Mrs. Durr -- Ruth to her friends -- is ELEGANT! Plumpish to the right amount, nice features, and Ma calls her auburn haired, whatever that means.

She wears crinolines most of the time, not in bed, I suppose, and the Guv says that she looks like a figure in Dresden china. Good skin, too, you know. Like porcelain, get me, Feef?" "I do indeed, Miss Ku, most graphic, thank you," I answered. "She sells books and things and although she is really Dutch she sells books in England. She is selling the Guv's books. We like her, we hope to see more of her now that we are going to live in Windsor city."

We sat for a moment in contemplation of Mrs. Durr's virtues, then it occurred to me to ask, "And has she any cat family?" Miss Ku clouded over. "Ah! I'm sorry you asked me that, it is a very sad case indeed, VERY sad." She paused and I am sure I heard her sniff a few times. Soon she got control of her emotions again and continued, "Yes, she has Stubby, who is a Tom that can't and he is a Queen as well who can't either. There was a dreadful mistake; poor Stubby is all mixed up in his, or her, Vital Department. But he has a heart of gold, yes, a heart of gold. Kindest person you could meet. Shy, very reserved as one would expect of one in his condition. The poor fellow would make a good mother to some homeless kitten; I must speak to the Guv about it."

"Is there a Mister Durr," I queried, then added, "of course there must be or she would not be Mrs." "Oh yes, there is a Mr.

Durr, he makes the milk for Windsor, without him everyone would be thirsty. He is Dutch too, so that makes the daughter Double Dutch I think. Yes Feef, you will like Mrs. Durr, she is worth purring at. But we have no time to discuss such things now, we have to arrange about the house.

Next week we shall move and I told the Guv I would see that you were not frightened." "I shall not be frightened, Miss Ku," I replied, "I have moved around quite a lot." "Well," said Miss Ku, ignoring my remarks, "next week the luggage and things will be taken in a truck and Ma will be there to see the things in. Soon after, the Guv will take you, Buttercup and me, and when we are settled the Guv and Ma will return here in order to see that everything is all right, clean and all that, and will take the key to the landlord."

By now the snows were melting, and the ice in the lake was breaking up and floating down the river. Sudden snow- storms reminded us that the summer was not yet upon us, but we could sense that the worst was over. Living in Canada was amazingly expensive, everything was twice -- or more -- the cost that it would have been in Ireland or France. The Guv tried to get work in the writing or television world. He found by bitter experience that firms in Canada do not want settlers unless they were (as the Guv put it) BUCK NAVVIES! Finding that he could not get into writing or television he tried anything, and found again that he was not wanted. None of us liked Canada, there was a remarkable lack of culture, a remarkable lack of appreciation of the finer things of life. I consoled myself with the thought that soon summer would be here and we would all feel better. The Guv, Buttercup, and Miss Ku went for a ride one day, I think they went to a shop in order to get a supply of peat moss. Ma and I made the beds and did a few odd jobs about the house. The stairs had to be dusted, and the old news- papers put aside. By the time we had done that they were back. "What d'ye think, Feef?" asked Miss Ku, coming across to me and whispering into an ear.

"What? Miss Ku," I replied, "What has happened?" "My Oh! My! You'll never guess," muttered Miss Ku, "You'll never guess. This will KILL you. She has met a man named Heddy who loves monkeys." "Monkeys, Miss Ku, you don't mean that we are going to have a monkey again!" Miss Ku laughed cynically, "No, Feef, we are not going to have A monkey, we are going to have TWO of the little horrors. Guess we shall have to swim for it with two of the things working overtime in the floods department." She sat silent for a moment, then said, "But perhaps they will be kept in the sun porch, we could not have two wild monkeys racing around. Monkeyrouse could not walk, these two are in good working order, guaranteed, satisfaction or refund of money." She exhaled gustily and said, "Buttercup is going to see the man Heddy soon, she LOVES monkeys!" "Most strange," I remarked, "Monkeys have such a bad reputation, I remember one in France, it was the pet of a retired seaman and it escaped one day and almost wrecked a fruit shop. I did not see it, mind, a lady named Madame Butterball told me about it, she ran a veterinary hospital. When I was a patient there she told me the history of the cage's last occupant, that monkey who cut himself by falling through a showcase."

We were busy packing, so many things had to be put into cases, Miss Ku and I worked overtime stamping on things to make them take up less space in the trunks. At times we had to rake things out of a packed case in order to make sure that nothing had been forgotten. We had to scrump up tissue paper, because everyone knows that scrumped up tissue is softer than the stiff new stuff. We worked very hard indeed, and I am proud to think that we helped so much. We particularly adored making clean sheets ready for use. No one likes sheets straight from the laundry, stiff and unfriendly, Miss Ku and I worked out a special system of running up and down the sheets until they were soft and pliable and no longer had the hard folds of freshly ironed sheets.

"Sheelagh!" Ma was calling from the kitchen, "the Carpenter is here to see about the monkey cage." "I'm coming," called Buttercup, clattering down the stairs. Miss Ku grunted in disdain. "Monkey cage, eh? That is going to cost a packet! Blow me, I don't know what things are coming to. We should go and listen, can't know too much." "Ya, ya," the Carpenter was saying, "the cage you vant heem in sections, no? Ya? I get heem quick. Vor de monks my vife she like to see, no ? I breeng her? Ya? I come." Miss Ku was chuckling to herself, "As soon as he said 'I come' he went, Feef. My! What a whacker this cage is going to be, the Guv, Ma, Buttercup and we could all get in together." "Will there be room at the new house, Miss Ku?" I asked. "Yeah! Yeah! Plenty of room, we shall have a big upstairs porch which is completely netted in. I thought we would have it as a playroom, instead it will be Monk Hall, as well! That's the way the cookies crumble!"

So the last few days dragged on. The Guv and Buttercup went to see Mister the Dutch Carpenter and came back with the news that the cage was finished and was being erected at the new house. With each trip that the Guv made to Windsor, more and more things were taken. Miss Ku went to see that everything was all right and came back to say, "Well, Feef, tomorrow you shall sleep in the City of Windsor, where we can look across and see the sights of Detroit. Some sights they are, too, some of them come over here in their flashy cars. Still, they bring dollars into the country. Good for trade and all that."

The Guv picked me up and we played together for a time. I loved to play with him, he would have a thin stick with something that rattled on the end, and as he drew it along the floor I could chase it by sound. Of course he let me catch it very often, just to give me confidence. I KNEW he was letting me catch the stick, but I pretended to him that I did not. This evening he ruffled my fur and stroked my chest.

"Early to bed, Feef, for we have a busy day tomorrow."

"Goodnight" said Ma and Buttercup, "Goodnight," we replied, then I heard the click of the light switch as the Guv turned it off for the last time in this house. Tomorrow? Tomorrow was another day, and would take us to another house. For tonight, I lay down and slept.

Chapter Ten

"Heigh Ho!" sang Miss Ku, "So off again we go. We travel round the world so large, like a Tomcat on a barge. We motor to this Windsor City, to move again would be" "Ah! Be quiet, Ku," said the Guv, "A fellow can't think with you trying to sing. Resign yourself to it, you are no more musica than I am." I smiled to myself. It was morning, and Miss Ku was greeting a long-past dawn with song. As the Guv spoke to her she wandered off, muttering," "You don't appreciate Art, that's what you don't!"

I stretched lazily, soon we would have breakfast. Already Ma was bustling about in the kitchen. The clatter of dishes came to my ears, then, "Ku! Feef! Come and have your breakfast!" "Coming, Ma," I replied as I felt for the edge of the bed and jumped off on to the floor. It was always an adventure, that getting off the bed in the morning. One's senses and perceptions are not so acute when one is barely awake, and I always had a mild fear that I might jump in the Guv's shoes or something. It was a very mild fear, though, because exceptional care was taken that I should come to no harm.

"Feef's coming!" called the Guv to Ma. "Come and get your breakfast, Feef," said Ma, "you are doping about like an old Granny this morning!" I smiled up at her and sat down to breakfast. "No, a bit more to the right -- that's it!" said Miss Ku.

"What shall we take next?" asked the Guv, "I am going to get the mail." Ma suggested which things were the most fragile, and the Guv and Buttercup carried them to the car. We had a mail box in Windsor, because we found that when people had our address they just called unexpectedly, and that made complications as the Guv would never see anyone who just called and demanded admittance. Miss Ku told me that when The Family lived in Ireland -- before I appeared on the scene -- a woman arrived from Germany and DEMANDED instant admittance as she "wanted to sit at the feet of the Lama." Told that she could not enter, she had actually camped on the doorstep until ordered to move by Mr. Loftus, looking very fierce and martial in his smart uniform.

Moving was a matter which did not concern Miss Ku and me. Soon the men from the removal firm had loaded our things and driven off. Miss Ku wandered around the house saying goodbye to the rooms. This was a parting of which we were glad, for this house had never felt friendly. Eventually Miss Ku and I were carried, well wrapped, to the warm car.

The Guv locked the house doors and we drove off. The road was bad, very bad, like so many Canadian roads, Miss Ku told me that there was a sign reading, "Broken road, drive at your own risk!" We drove on and came to a crossing. Miss Ku called out, "That is where our food came from, Feef, a place called 'Stop n'shop.' Now we are on the main Windsor road." The going was smoother here. My nose wrinkled at a sudden familiar odor, an odor which reminded me of Mister the Irish Vet and his Irish Cat Hospital. Miss Ku laughed, "Don't be such a sissy, Feef, this is just a human hospital where they take people who are just about finished." We drove on a little and she said, "And here is where motor cars are made, we are passing the Ford factory. I'll tell you all, Feef, I'll give you the gen."

"Miss Ku!" I called, "What a strange smell, in some vague way it reminds me of the French vineyards, yet it is a DIFFERENT smell." "Sure it is," said Miss Ku, "Here is a factory where they make drink stuff Grain which could feed starving people is mashed up to make a drink of sorts which people would be better without. But we are going over a rail- road bridge now, every train from anywhere to Windsor passes under this bridge." We drove on a little and then there was such a resounding

CRASH! that I leaped straight into the air. "Don't be a slob, Feef," said Miss Ku, "that was just an engine shunting." The Guv turned the car, and stopped.

"Home, Feef," said Ma. Miss Ku and I were carried across the snow- covered path, through the front door and up the stairs. There was the strong smell of fresh varnish and soap. I sniffed the floor and decided that it had recently been well polished. "Never mind that," said Miss Ku, "you can deal with the floor later. I am going to take you from room to room and tell you about the place. Pay attention because we have some new furniture." "Sheelagh!" called the Guv, "We are going to deliver the keys to the landlord, Shan't be long."

The Guv and Ma went out, I heard them going down the stairs, get into the car and drive off. "Well, now come with me," said Miss Ku.

We went all through the Apartment, Miss Ku pointing out obstacles, and the whereabouts of chairs. Then we went out to the back porch. "Open up, please!" yelled Miss Ku. "Do you want to go out, Ku?" asked Buttercup, "All right, I will open the door." She walked across the kitchen and opened the door. A blast of cold air rushed in and we rushed out.

"Here," said Miss Ku, "is the upstairs sun porch. Screened on three sides. Shortly it will be Monkey Hall. It will be heated. Brr! Let's get out, it is too cold here." We wandered into the kitchen, and Buttercup shut the porch door with a sigh of relief and another sigh for silly cats who wandered around -- to her -- aimlessly!

"Here is the bedroom you will share with the Guv. It looks out over the railroad, over the Detroit River and Detroit City. In the summer, so I am told, ships from all over the world come past this window. We shall see, we shall see!"

Miss Ku was in her element, describing the view. "Slightly to the left of us is the place where some men dug a hole beneath the River and made a roadway to America, further left is the Ambassador Bridge. Guv says the word Detroit is a corruption of the French for 'The Straits'. Guess you'll know all about that, Feef!" Miss Ku suddenly swiveled round so fast that her tail swept across my face. "Golly!" she breathed, "some horrible looking man is staring up at me, he is carrying an official looking briefcase, too."

That night we slept fitfully, disturbed a lot by the rattle and crash of trains past the window. In the morning Ma went down the stairs to collect the milk. She returned with the milk and a letter which she handed to the Guv. "What's this?" he asked. "I don't know," said Ma, "It was in the box." There was the sound of an envelope being ripped open, and then silence as the Guv read. "My goodness!" he exclaimed, "Is there NO limit to the foolishness of Canadian officials?

Listen to this. This is a letter from the Department of National Revenue. It starts:

"Dear Sir,

Information received by this office indicates that you are making rental payments to a non-resident of Canada and are not withholding tax. Since you have failed to withhold tax since May 1st, 1959, you are required to withhold sufficient monies from your next rental payment to cover the amount of tax which should have been withheld.

"If you fail to withhold tax as required by the Income Tax Acts, you will be penalized in accordance with..."

"You see?" said the Guv, "we moved in yesterday and already we get threats. I wish we could wake up as from a nightmare and find that we were back in dear old Ireland. WHY do these immature Canadians threaten and bluster so? I think I will take the whole matter up with officials in Ottawa."

Miss Ku nudged me, "You see, Feef. Just as I told you, that horrible man yesterday was a tax, spy. I saw him." We listened, the Guv was still talking about it. "Can't understand this country, they threaten me with deportation in the very first letter they sent me. Instead of asking me to go to the Medical Officer of Health they THREATEN me with deportation if I don't go. Now, the very day after we move in, they threaten all sorts of penalties. People of this country have not the wits to know that the Wild West days are over."

"The Guv is getting wild," whispered Miss Ku, "we should hide under the bed!"

The days slipped smoothly by. Gradually we became accustomed to the noises of the trains. The Guv made an awful fuss about the threatening letters, and received apologies from the local Tax people and also from the Ottawa government. A piece appeared in the newspapers about the Canadian officials who tried to intimidate settlers! The weather became warmer and Miss Ku and I were able to sit on the balcony and play in the garden downstairs.

One morning the Guv came back from the Walkerville Post Office with quite a lot of mail, as usual, but this day in particular he brought a very nice letter from Mrs. O'Grady. "I miss her," said Ma, "I wish she could come out and see us." The Guv sat still for a time, then he said, "She was a good friend to us. Why don't we get her to come?" Ma and Buttercup sat, silent with amazement. "Guv's gone off his head at last," whispered Miss Ku, "that's what Canada has done to him." "Rab," said the Guv, "how about writing to Mrs. O'Grady and asking if she would like to come? Tell her if she comes next month she will be here the same time as the Queen of England. Think of that, the Queen of England, and Mrs. O'Grady of Eire here at the same time. Tell her the Queen will pass up the River right in front of us. Tell her FOR PETE'S SAKE let us know soon!"

Miss Ku, with quite unconscious humor, said, "Well Feef, now that we have finally got rid of the monkeys we are going to have Mrs. O'Grady." We all LOVED Mrs. O'Grady, and counted her as a very true friend." I laughed, and pointed out that Miss Ku made it appear that 'Ve O'G' was in the same class as the monkeys. Miss Ku, with her usual wit, turned it back on me with, "Nonsense, Feef, anyone but you would realize that after the storm comes the sunshine.

Mrs. O'Grady is the sunshine after the monkey storm." The monkeys had been a 'storm' as I heartily agreed. Soon after we had moved into the Riverside Drive house, Mister the Dutch Carpenter had arrived with a truck and the cage. "I vant vor do bring mine Vife vor do see der monkeys, yaas?" he said. Buttercup, the Monkey Queen, said yes, he could bring his 'vife' for to see der monkeys when they were installed. Mister the Dutch Carpenter and Mister the Dutch Carpenter's son carried up all the pieces and worked mightily, well, not TOO mightily, to assemble the affair.

Then they rubbed their hands, stood back, and waited for the dollars. That settled, they went off after assurances that Missus the Dutch Carpenter's Wife should be invited to Monkey Hall. . .
.

A day or so later two monkeys arrived, in a big basket of course. Buttercup, all agog to see them, incautiously opened the lid a fraction too much. "OW!" yelled Miss Ku, "DIVE BENEATH THE BED, Feef, WILD MONKEYS ARE LOOSE!" We dived beneath the bed so that we should not be in the way or impede the monkey hunt. The Guv, Ma, and Buttercup dashed around the rooms, shutting windows and doors. For a time all was madness. It seemed that hordes of monkeys were racing around. Miss Ku said, "I will stay near the wall, Feef, and then I shall be safe to grab you and pull you back if a monkey reaches in for you."

At last one monkey was caught and put in the cage, and then after further struggles, the second. The Family sat back and mopped bedewed brows. Soon Buttercup rose to her feet and formed herself into a one- woman Sanitary Corps to go round the house and remove Monkey Trademarks which were distributed everywhere with amazing profusion. As Miss Ku wisely remarked, "My Golly! I'm glad these things don't fly, Feef!" The Guv and Ma went round straightening things and helping to restore the place to its pre-monkey state.

The Monkey Experiment was not a success. The noise, the smell, the general commotion which the creatures caused was too much. A frantic plea went out to the man called Heddy. "Yes," he agreed, "these wild monkeys from the South American forests were not really suitable for private homes, but only for zoos." He would take the monkeys, he said, and let us have a tame one, one bred in captivity, and suitable for a pet. A pale and shaken Family said, unanimously, "NO! Just take these back. Take the cage too as good measure!" So, two monkeys and one very large specially made cage went back. Miss Ku and I now strode about the house with greater confidence, no longer constantly on the alert for monkeys which might have escaped. When the smell had abated, and after the sun porch had been thoroughly washed several times, we spent much time out there. It was a pleasant spot, where the sun shone upon us in the mornings and where we could smell flowers and growing things from the gardens nearby. We had many laughs about the monkeys, but only in retrospect, only in retrospect!

Our joy at the departure of the monkeys was soon increased by a letter from Mrs. O'Grady. Yes, she would come, she wrote, her Husband was glad she would have such an opportunity to travel. "What was he?" I whispered to Miss Ku, "He was a very important man," she whispered back, "he used to be the Voice of a Ship and used to speak so that all the world could hear. Then he was called Sparks." Miss Ku thought a moment and then added, "I think he was something to do with radio, yes, it must be, he makes all the electricity for Dublin now, it figgers -- it figgers!" "Have they any family, Miss Ku?" I queried. "Yeah, sure," she replied, "they have a girl kitten called Doris -- she will be coming as well -- and Mr. Samuel Dog who looks after the place. He is nearly as old as you, Feef."

The weeks slipped by. One morning the Guv called Miss Ku and me and said, "Now Cats, the next week is going to be busy and noisy. The Queen of England is coming to Windsor, there will be bands and fireworks. Mrs. O'Grady and Doris will arrive today. You, Ku, you must look after Feef; I am going to make you responsible for Feef's safety." "Okay Guv, Okay!" said Miss Ku, "Don't I always look after her as if she were my own great great grandmother?" There was much preparation, Ma and Buttercup used extra elbow grease on the place, the Guv and we cats used extra energy keeping out of the way so that we should not be swept up.

"Let's go up in the attic," said Miss Ku at last. "These women with their flap make the place dangerous to live in." The weather was hot, terribly hot. Miss Ku and I found it hard work to even breathe. Just as our first winter in Canada was exceptionally cold, so was this, the hot season, exceptionally hot. As Miss Ku said, "Golly! Feef, you just can't have raw food now, everything is cooked by this weather." Ma had gone to Montreal the day before so that she could fly back with Mrs. O'Grady. At about one o'clock of "arrival day" the Guv got out the big car and drove off to Windsor Airport. Buttercup bumbled around and kept looking out of the window. Miss Ku said there was much to see. Within a very few days there would be processions, bands, and aeroplane fly-overs. Not for Mrs. O'Grady, Miss Ku made clear, but for the English Queen who was in the district. There were going to be firework displays, which I knew meant many big bangs. But now we were waiting for our friend Mrs. O'Grady.

Miss Ku and I were having a light lunch in order to fortify ourselves. Buttercup was peering out of the window. Suddenly she said, Ah Here they are!" (she said it in English as she did not speak Cat), and then she ran down the stairs to open the front door. "You keep out of the way, Feef," said Miss Ku. "Young Daughter Kittens may be a bit clumsy with their feet. ALL humans are," she said as an afterthought "You keep close to me and I will see you are all right."

There was much commotion on the stairs, chattering and laughing, and the sound of cases being dropped on the floor. "Golly!" whispered Miss Ku, "Poor old Ve O'G is looking as hot as a newly fried rasher of bacon. Hope she survives!"

At last they reached the top of the stairs and Mrs. O'Grady flopped in the nearest chair. When she had recovered somewhat Ma said, "Come out on the balcony, it may be cooler there." We all trooped out, and sat down. For some time the talk was of Ireland, a subject dear to the heart of the Guv and Ma. Then the talk swung to the English Queen, a subject dear to the heart of Buttercup, but which left the Guv un- moved. Miss Ku said, "If you want to talk of Queens, WE are the best Queens you will ever meet!" Mrs. O'Grady was looking hotter and hotter. At last she retired to the lower Apartment where she cooled off in Best Windsor City Water and eventually returned looking a little refreshed. Ma had arranged for Mrs. O'Grady and Daughter to stay at a very good Hotel, the Metropole, and after they had stopped long enough to see the lights of Detroit, the Guv and Ma drove them to the Hotel. Miss Ku went to show the Guv the way, and tell him the best way to drive. I suppose they were gone for half an hour, then the Guv, Ma and Miss Ku returned and we all went to bed to rest in preparation for another day.

In the morning Ma said, "We will collect them after breakfast, when we go for the mail. I think we should drive them round Windsor so they know what sort of a place it is." We had our breakfast, then Miss Ku and I helped the Guv dress. He is very sick, you see, and has had enough troubles to finish anyone. Now he has to rest a lot and take great care. Miss Ku and I have devoted our lives to looking after him.

Soon he and Ma went down the back stairs and across the garden to the garage. Our Landlady lived in Detroit, but in Windsor her affairs were well looked after by her cousin, a very pleasant lady who always spoke most politely to Miss Ku and me. We all Liked her a lot. Our car was too large to enter the garage of our house, so Miss Landlady's Cousin let. us keep it in her garage which was very, very large indeed.

Yes, she was a very pleasant woman indeed and talked to us a lot. I remember that one day she told us that within the life-time of her father all the settlers worked with guns beside them because of the very real threat of Indian raids. Her. father, she told us, took his cattle to drink from the River, where now the railroad tracks run. She had another house a very few miles from Windsor which was a real Log Cabin made of walnut logs. Miss Ku went to see it once and was very impressed with the strange creatures living beneath the steps.

"Glorious Grasshoppers!" said Miss Ku, "they ARE a long time!" We thought that it was a waste of time to sit and wait, so we went up into the attic and did our nails on the beams and had a nice cool dust-bath. From the topmost ridge of the house Miss Ku looked down into the street, some forty feet away. "They have come," she called, and dropped lightly to the attic floor. Racing down the stairs we were just in time to greet them as they came in. The Guv picked me up and put me across his shoulder and carried me up the stairs.

Miss Ku ran ahead up the stairs, calling to Buttercup to come and say "Good morning, Visitors."

"We went down to see the British Destroyers," said the Guv. "They are moored down by Dieppe Park. We also took a trip round the city. Now Mrs. O'Grady wants to sit and re- cover from the heat." We took chairs and went out on to the balcony. Mrs. O'Grady was very interested indeed in the sights of the River, with ships from all over the world passing along before her eyes. The Guv talked about some Seaway and said that that was the reason for the presence of the ships.

I did not at all understand it, and Miss Ku was very vague, but it appeared that some humans had dug a ditch to let water from the Great Lakes flow faster to the sea. As certain American cities were taking too much water, locks were installed and some Canadians kept the keys. They had to unlock some water in order that a ship could float in, then they locked a door behind and unlocked another in front. It was all mysterious to Miss Ku and me, but the Guv knew about it and he told Mrs. O'Grady who seemed to understand what it was all about.

A few days went by, with The Family taking Mrs. O'Grady about to see the sights. It appeared to me to be a waste of time as Miss Ku said they passed by our window. "Gee! Feef!" she would exclaim, "Look at that woman, isn't she a sight?" There was much activity about in front of our house, men were putting up decorations and putting down containers for litter. Little boats with officious men roared along the water, yelling loudly in order to show their importance.

Crowds of people came and sat on the railroad tracks, looking out across the water, and throngs of stationary cars jammed the roads. The Family sat on the balcony. The Guv did a lot of photography, and on this day he had a three-legged thing with a camera on the top. On the camera he had what Miss Ku called a telephoto powerful enough to photograph a cat in Detroit.

Mrs. O'Grady was fidgeting about on her chair. "Look!" she exclaimed with great excitement, "all the American shore is lined by red-coated Canadian Mounties!" Miss Ku stifled a laugh as the Guv replied, "No, Mrs. O'Grady, they are not Mounties, that is a train loaded with red-painted farm tractors which have been exported from Canada." As Miss Ku said, it DID look like red-coated troops, so anyone at all could be excused from such an innocent mistake.

More ships were coming up the River. The noise of the crowd was temporarily hushed, then a babble of talk and a few cheers broke out. "There she is," said Ma, "standing alone on the after deck." "And there is the Prince," said Buttercup, "more towards the center of the ship." "I got a fine photo of that helicopter," said the Guv, "a man was leaning out and photographing the ships below him. That will make a good picture" The ships went away up the River and as the last vessel moved out of sight the cars on the road started up again. The crowds dispersed and, as Miss Ku said, all that was left to remind us was about half a ton of litter.

Once again the train ferries crossed and recrossed the River,and trains thundered and hooted along the tracks before our windows.

While there was yet light, some barges were towed out into the River and positioned on the water where Canada became America, and America became Canada. Apparently if the fireworks were to be discharged from that position, both countries, and not just one, would be responsible for any damage caused. Once again the crowds collected, bringing eatables and drinkables -- particularly the latter -- with them. All the trains stopped, and someone must have told the ships that they could not come any further. At last the Fire- work Hour arrived. Nothing happened. More time passed; and still nothing happened. A man called out and said that one of the Set Pieces had fallen in the water. Eventually there came a few weak bangs, not really loud enough to frighten a new-born kitten, and Miss Ku said there were a few strange lights in the sky. Then it was all over. The Guv and Ma said it was time to take Mrs. O'Grady back to the Hotel. Ma said "We will get a taxi, we shall never get our car out of the garage with a crowd like this." She called the taxi companies and was told that all taxis were held up in traffic jams.

"There are a million people or more on the water front," she was told, "and traffic is packed solid." The Guv got out the car, and he, Ma, and Mrs. O'Grady disappeared into the crowd. More than an hour later the Guv and Ma returned and said that they had taken an hour to do two miles. The next day the Guv and Ma took Mrs. O'Grady to see the sights of Detroit, they drove around a lot and then came back to Miss Ku and me. Mrs. O'Grady said she wanted to do some shopping over there so she, Ma and Buttercup all went together, leaving Miss Ku and me to look after the Guv.

This was a very full, a very busy week, with two or three weeks sightseeing crammed into one. All too soon the aeroplane people had to fly a plane back to Ireland, to Shannon from whence we had set out.

The Guv and Ma drove Mrs. O'Grady and Daughter to the Airport at Windsor. As we heard Ma tell Buttercup later, they waited until the plane actually took off The O'Grady's were starting off on a journey, back to Ireland, which we wished we could do. The Guv had tried hard to get work in Windsor, or in Canada. He was willing to go anywhere at all in the country. All he was ever offered was a job as a manual laborer, and that was just too silly for words. Canada, we are agreed, is a most uncultured country, and all of us live for the day when we can leave it. However, this book is not a treatise on the faults of Canada that would fill a complete library, anyway!

Miss Ku and I were often able to go out in the garden now, never alone of course, because of the many dogs in the district. Siamese cats are not afraid of dogs, but humans are afraid of what WE could do to the dogs. We have been known to jump on the back of an attacking dog, sink in claws, and ride him like a human rides a horse. Apparently it was permissible for humans to strap steel spikes on their heels and then tear a horse's sides with them, but if we sank our claws into a dog in self defense WE were termed "savage."

This afternoon was a pleasant one; we sat together beneath the Guv's chair -- he is very big, weighing two hundred and twenty five pounds and needs a big chair -- when a whole collection of cars went by with horns shrieking the place down. I had never bothered about it before, thinking it was just Canadians, so there did not have to be any sense in things they did. I happened to say, "Miss Ku, I wonder why they make all this noise?" Miss Ku was very erudite, and being sighted she had a great advantage over me. "I'll tell you, Feef," she replied. "Over here when a Tom and a Queen human gets married, they stick ribbons on the cars and then drive in procession with horns blaring all the time. I think it is meant to say, 'Look out! A gang of crackpots is coming!' " She settled herself more comfortably and added, "And when a human dies and is being taken to be shoved into a hole in the ground all the funeral cars keep their head- lights full on and have blue and white flags marked 'funeral' flying from the side of the cars. They have right of way over all traffic and do not have to stop for traffic lights."

"That is MOST interesting, Miss Ku, MOST interesting," I said.

Miss Ku chewed a blade of grass for a few moments, then said, "I could tell you a lot about Canada. Here, for instance, when a human dies they take the body off to a Funeral Home, fix him or her up -- embalming they call it -- do up the face with paints, and put 'em on show in their coffins, or caskets as they are called over here. Then a party calls to pay the 'last respects' ' Sometimes a body will be half sitting up in the casket. The Guv says these Funeral Homes are the biggest money making racket ever. Then when people are going to get married their friends give them a shower." Miss Ku stopped and chuckled. "When I heard that first, Feef," she smiled, "I thought the friends gave them a bath -- you know, a shower bath. But no, it means they are showered with gifts. Mainly things they don't want, or things which EVERYONE gives them. What would a bride do with half a dozen coffee percolators?" She sighed, "It is a crazy country, anyhow," she said, "Same with the children. Don't do a thing to the dear little children, don't be cross with them, have special Guards to escort them across the roads. Treat 'em as if they have no brains of their own, which is fair enough, but the point is -- the day they leave school for the last time, they are on their own. No one looks after them then.

Over here, Feef, there is the unhealthy Cult of the Human Kitten. They can do no wrong. Bad for them, Feef, bad fo the country. They should have discipline, or in later years they will fall into crime through being treated too softly when young. Kids here are creeps, punks, BAH!" I nodded in sympathy. Miss Ku was quite right. Indulge a kitten too much, and you laid the foundation for a dissatisfied adult.

The Guv stood up, "If you cats want to stay here longer," he said, "I will go upstairs and get the camera. I want to photograph these roses." The Guv was a very keen photographer, and had a wonderful collection of color slides. He turned and went up the stairs to get his good Japanese Topcon Camera. "Pssst!" whispered the cat from Across the Road, "Psst! I got sumting to tell you, Lady Ku'ei, will ya come to th' fence?" Miss Ku rose to her feet and sauntered across to the wire mesh fence at the side of the garden. She and the cat from Across the Road whispered for a time, then Miss Ku returned and sat by me again. "He only wanted to brief me on the latest American slang," she said, "nothing important." The Guv came out with his camera in order to photograph the flowers. Miss Ku and I retreated under some bushes, for we HATED to have our photographs taken. We hated to be stared at by curious sightseers, too. Miss Ku had a mortifying memory of a stupid Canadian woman poking her nose in the car window, pointing to Miss Ku and saying, "What is it, a

MONKEY?" Poor Miss Ku went hot all over every time she thought of it!

That night, it was a Saturday, there were many people about. There was some sort of a party on at the Drink House a little distance up the road. Cars were roaring around, and there was much loud talk and discussion as men tried to bargain with women who were waiting on the streets. We went to bed, Buttercup in a room to the side of the house, where she had photographs of monkeys and human kittens and the statue of a Bulldog named Chester. Ma and Miss Ku had a nice room facing the front of the house, and the Guv and I slept in a room facing the front too, facing Detroit and the River. Soon I heard the Guv click off the light, and the bed creaked as he settled down. I sat for a time on the broad window sill, picking up the sounds of the busy night, thinking? What was I thinking? Well, I was comparing the hard past with the lovely present, thinking that, as the Old Tree had said, I was now Home, wanted, living in peace and happiness. Now, because I knew I could do anything, or go anywhere in the house, I took particular care to do nothing that could offend even Mme. Diplomat in far-off France. I remembered the Gov's motto, "Do as you would be done by." A warm glow of happiness engulfed me. The Guv was breathing gently and I walked across his bed to make sure that he was all right. I curled up at the foot of his bed and fell asleep.

Suddenly I was acutely awake. The night was still except for the faintest of scratchings. A mouse? I listened for a time. The scratching continued. There came the muffled sound of breaking wood. Quickly I jumped silently off the bed and crept across the room in search of Miss Ku. She entered the room and whispered, "Sa-ay; I got noos for ya, ya'd better believe it! I learned that today from the Cat Across the Road. There is a BURGLAR downstairs, shall we go and rip his throat out?" I thought for a moment, Siamese Cats do do such things in defense of property, but then I thought that we were supposed to be civilized, so I said, "No, I think we should call the Guv, Miss Ku." "Oh goody, yes!" she exclaimed, "He will soon knock Seven Bells out of a burglar." I jumped on the bed and gently patted the Guv on the shoulder. He stretched out a hand and rubbed my chin.

"What is it, Feef?" he asked. Miss Ku jumped up and sat on his chest, "Hey, Guv, a BURGLAR is breaking in. Beat him up!" The Guv listened a moment, then silently reached for his slippers and dressing gown. Picking up a powerful torch that stood nearby, he crept down the stairs, Miss Ku and I following him. Buttercup came out of her room, "What's happening?" she asked. "Sssh! Burglars," said the Guv, continuing down the stairs. Beneath us the scratching had stopped. Miss Ku shouted, "THERE HE IS!" I heard pounding footsteps and the crash of the garden gate. By now Ma and Buttercup had joined the Guv. We all went through the lower Apartment. A stiff breeze was blowing through an opened window. "Gerhumping Golliwogs!" exclaimed Miss Ku in awe, "The guy has broken out the window frame!"

The Guv dressed and went outside to nail up the broken woodwork. We did not call the Police. Once before a gang of children had stolen the back gate. Ma phoned the Police, and when at long last a policeman came he said, "Aw, you're lucky they did not take the roof from over your heads."

We Siamese Cats have a high sense of responsibility. In Tibet we guard the Temples, and we guard also those whom we love even when it costs us our life. Here is another of our legends.

Centuries and centuries ago there lived an old man who was the Keeper of the Wilds to an ancient Lamasery in the far far East. He Lived deep in a forest, sharing his cave home with a small Siamese Queen cat who had seen much of the sorrows of life. Together the old Keeper, who was venerated as a Saint, and the little Siamese Cat trod the forest paths, she keeping a respectful distance behind him. Together they went in search of animals who were ill, or hungry, bringing comfort to those afflicted and aid to those with broken limbs.

One night the old Keeper, who was a Monk really, retired to his bed of leaves, exhausted by an unusually tiring day. The little old cat curled up close by. Soon they were fast asleep, fearing no danger, for they were the friends of all the animals. Even the savage wart-hog and the tiger respected and loved the Keeper and the Cat.

During the darkest hours of the night, a poisonous snake, with evil intent, crawled into the cave. Jealous, and with the insane evil that only a poisonous snake could display, it slithered on to the sleeping Monk's leafy bed and was about to strike him with poisoned fangs. Leaping to her feet, the Cat jumped on the back of the snake's neck, distracting its attention from the now awakened Keeper. The battle was long and fierce, with the snake writhing and squirming across the length and breadth of the cave. At last, almost collapsing from exhaustion, the Cat bit through the spinal column of the snake which soon became still in death.

Gently the old Monk disengaged the little Cat from the monstrous folds of the dead snake. Cuddling her in his arms, he said, "Little Cat, for long you and your kind have guarded us and our Temples. You shall always have your place in the homes, the hearths, and the hearts of man. From now on our Destinies shall be joined."

I thought of all this as we trooped back to our bedrooms and lay down to sleep. The Guv reached out and lovingly tweaked my ears, then rolled over and fell asleep.

Chapter Eleven

"Feef!" Miss Ku came running up the stairs in a great state of agitation. "Feef," she exclaimed as she reached the top and came into the room, "The Old Man's gone off his head!" She muttered to herself glumly as she dashed into the kitchen to get some food. The Guv had gone off his head? I could not understand what she meant, I knew that he had taken Miss Ku for a drive to Riverside. Now, after being out for rather more than an hour, Miss Ku said he had gone off his head! I jumped up to the window sill and thought about it. In the River a ship hooted the signal which the Guv had told us meant "I am turning to port."

There was the soft patter of small feet, and Miss Ku jumped lightly up to sit beside me. "He's got a rock in his head the size of the Hill of Howth, she said as she carefully washed herself. "But Miss Ku," I expostulated, "What has happened? HOW has the Guv gone off his head?" "Ow!" she replied, "we were driving along so peacefully and suddenly the Old Man got a Bee in his Bonnet. He stopped the car and looked at the engine. 'Don't like the sound of it,' he said, 'I know that something is going to happen.' Ma was sitting there like a Stuffed Duck, saying nothing. He got in the car again and as we drove off he said, 'We will take Ku home and then go on to the garage and see what other cars they have.' So here am I, dumped in like a load of garbage while they go gallivanting off in my car!" She sat grumpily on the far edge of the sill, muttering to herself.

"Gee! Oh Golly!" Miss Ku jumped up and danced on the window sill in a frenzy of excitement. I, being blind, had no choice but to keep calm, for I did not know the cause of the excitement. "My!" she squealed, her voice becoming higher and higher, "It's real cute, real smart, a smashing automobile! White and pink." I sat still, waiting for her to calm down and tell me what was happening. Just then I heard a car door shut and seconds later the Guv and Ma came up the stairs, "New car, eh?" asked Buttercup. "Good!" I thought, "now I shall get the story." "Yes, another car, a Mercury," said the Guv. "Only one owner, and a low mileage. A really good car. I think the camshaft is going to give trouble on the other. This one is on trial for the day, want to come out?" Miss Ku jumped to her feet and rushed to the door so that she at least would not be forgotten.

"Coming for a ride in the new car, Feef?" asked the Guv, rubbing my chin. "No thank you," I replied, "I will stay here with Ma and keep house." He told me I was an old stick-in-the-mud and then went on down the stairs. Miss Ku and Buttercup were already sitting in the car. I heard them start off, then Ma and I got the tea ready for when they returned.

Brrr. Brrr. Brrr. said the telephone. Ma hurried to answer it, because telephones do not like to be kept waiting. "Oh! Hello, Mrs. Durr," said Ma. She listened for a time -- I could hear the faint sounds from the telephone, not loud enough for me to comprehend, though. "He is out trying a different car. I'll tell him when he comes back," said Ma. She and Mrs. Durr talked for a time, then Ma went back to her work.

Soon we heard the Guv, Buttercup and Miss Ku coming up the back stairs after putting away the car. "Mrs. Durr phoned," said Ma. "Just a friendly call, but she has had some trouble, someone has let her down with the premises she was going to take."

We all liked Mrs. Durr. After working hard for another firm she was going to set up her own book shop which was to be called "Bookland", of Dorwin Plaza, Windsor. "She is in quite a state," said Ma, "she has nowhere to store the books and things until she can move into the new shop at Dorwin."

The Guv got on with his tea, saying nothing until he had finished, then, "How long would she want the place?" he asked. "A month, not more," said Ma. "Tell her to come round and see us. She can store all her things in the down- stair apartment for a month. We pay rent on it, the landlady can say nothing so long as no selling is done there." Ma went to the telephone and dialed the number. . . .

"There's Ruth!" called Miss Ku. "Ku!" said the Guv, "You are not a Canadian, calling everyone by their first name, she is Mrs. Durr." "Phooey!"said Miss Ku, "She is RUTH to me and the little Gentleman Siamese Kitten she has is Chuli, not Mr. Durr." Mrs. Durr came up the stairs at the front and we all said hello and then we all went down the backstairs to see the lower apartment. The Guv carried me on his shoulder because he thought there would be too many feet for me to avoid, as I could not see them. "Well there you are, Mrs. Durr," said the Guv, "You can store your things here and work here all day if you like. You CANNOT sell from here, and you cannot pay us any rent. Then the land- lady or Windsor City Council are powerless to object. There are no shops here as you know." Mrs. Durr seemed to be very pleased. She played with me, and I gave my second best purr, we always keep our very best purrs for The Family. I knew that Mr. Chuli Durr would be able to explain that to her when he became older. Then he was a small kitten indeed, with his face and tail still white. Now, at this time of writing, I understand that he is indeed a most magnificent specimen of Tom-hood. Miss Ku recently received a photograph from him and she described him gustily and in some detail.

The next morning loads and loads of books were carried in to the downstairs apartment. For most of the morning men seemed to be arriving with great boxes, and grunting mightily as they struggled to manhandle those cases in through the doors. Soon after lunch I heard more men come, "Telephone men;" said Miss Ku. "She has to have a tele- phone, doesn't she? ANY dope would know that!" There came the noise of hammering, and shortly after, the telephone bell rang as it was tested. "I'm going down to see everything is all right," said Miss Ku. "Wait a minute, Ku," said the Guv, "let the men finish and then we will all go down to see Mrs. Durr." It seemed to me that the best thing for me to do would be to have some food as I did not know how long we should be. I wandered off to the kitchen and was fortunate enough to discover Ma just putting down a fresh supply. I gave her a push with my head and rubbed against her legs by way of thanks. What a pity, I thought, that she does not yet speak Cat like the Guv does.

Not long after the Guv opened the kitchen door leading to the back stairs. Miss Ku rushed headlong down -- I could easily manage the stairs now, knowing each one and being well aware that there would be no obstacles. The Guv was VERY firm about that; he was fanatically particular to see that all my 'routes' were kept clear and that the furniture was always in the same place. I suppose that as the Guv had once been blind for just over a year he knew of my problems better than anyone else.

We rushed down the stairs and skidded to a halt outside Mrs. Durr's door. She opened it and welcomed us in.. I waited at the door for the Guv as I did not know of the obstacles. He picked me up and carried me in, placing me beside a big case so that I could sniff all the news. Some were rude messages left by dogs, other smells showed that the bottom of the box had rested on damp ground. On one book I read a message from Mr./ Miss Stubby Durr. He/She was very pleased at having Master Chuli Durr to look after, Miss Ku sighed a sigh of happy memories "Old Stubby, a very pleasant fellow or fellowess," she remarked, "Sad to say, something got mixed when the sexes were handed out, poor old Stubby had both. MOST embarrassing! I called at the Durr House one evening and could hardly keep my eyes off-- no, I mean, I didn't know where to look." "Yes, yes, Miss Ku," I said, "But I understand He/She has the sweetest of natures, and Mr. Chuli Durr will be well looked after."

Miss Ku went out a lot in the Mercury car, seeing all the local scenery, and going on to Leamington and places like that. I loved her to come back and tell me all about it, tell me of all the things I could no longer see for myself. One afternoon, when she returned, she was beaming with pleasure.

Nudging me, she said, "Come under the bed, Feef, I'll tell you all about it." I rose and followed her under the bed. Together we sat down, close to each other. Miss Ku started to wash, and as she washed she talked. "Well, Feef, we started out and we went all along the fast highway. We passed a lot of fruit and vegetable stands, where people were selling the stuff they had grown. Buttercup went 'Ooh!' and 'Ah!' at each one. But the Guv didn't stop. We drove on and on and then some more. We drove towards the lake and then we passed a factory where they made Fifty Seven Varieties of food! Think of that, Feef, think how YOU would like to be let loose in there!" I did think about it, and the more I thought about it the more sure I was that nothing -- nothing at all -- could be better than my present home. Fifty Seven Varieties of food perhaps, but here I also had ONE variety of love, the best. The mere thought of it made me purr. "Then we went and had a look at the lake," said Miss Ku, "and we saw that the water was just as wet as that at Windsor, so we turned for Home. At the fruit stands Buttercup went 'Ah!' and 'Ooh!' so the Guv stopped and she got out and bought some of those smelly things that go splash when they are bitten. She beamed all the way home and every so often touched the fruit smelly things and thought how she was going to get into them. Then we turned into Walkerville and picked up the mail and here we are."

"You cats should button up your ears," said the Guv, "Mrs. Durr is having her things moved out tomorrow, she now has the place finished at Dorwin Plaza." "OW!" yelled Miss Ku, "Will you take me to see it?" "Sure," said the Guv, "and Feef as well if she likes." We wandered down the stairs and knocked at the door. Mrs. Durr opened it and very civilly invited us in. We looked in all the rooms and sniffed round all the boxes of books which had been packed up ready for transfer to the new shop. "What did she unpack them for, Miss Ku?" I asked. "Why, you silly Old Woman Cat," said Miss Ku, "she had to look at them so she could check off her invoices and do something about a catalogue. ANY sensible cat would have known that. Anyhow, I watched her doing it" I went across to Mrs. Durr and rubbed against her to show her that I was sorry she had to work so hard. Then the Guv and Ma came down and we all went out into the garden to smell the roses.

The Guv and Ma were deep in discussion, some days later. "Costs in this country are so fantastically high that I shall HAVE to get a job." said the Guv. "You are not fit to," replied Ma. "No, but we have to live all the same. I will go to the Employment Exchange and see what they say. After all, I can write, I have been in Radio, and there are a whole lot of things I can do" He went out to get the car. Ma called after him, "Ku wants to go to Walkerville with us to get the mail." Soon after the Guv drove round to the front door and Ma went out carrying Miss Ku. She got in the car and off they went. Around about lunch time they returned looking glum.

"Come under the bed, Feef," whispered Miss Ku, "I will tell you what happened." I rose to my feet and walked to our Conference Place beneath the bed. When we were properly settled, Miss Ku said, "After we had been for the mail we drove down to the Employment Office. The Guv got out and went in. Ma and I sat together in the car. Much later the Guv came out looking really fed up with everything. He got in his car, started it, and drove off without saying a word. We drove to that place beneath the Ambassador Bridge -- you know, Feef-- where we took you. He stopped the car and said, 'I wish we could get out of this country!' 'What happened?' asked Ma. 'I went in,' said the Guv, 'and a clerk at the counter sniggered and made goat noises as he fingered an imaginary beard. I went up to another clerk and told him I wanted work. The man laughed and said I would get only laboring work the same as any other * * * * * * * D.P.' 'D.P?' asked Ma, 'What's that?' 'Displaced Person,' replied the Guv, 'these Canadians think they are God's Gift to the world, they think that anyone from another part of the world is an ex-convict or something. Well, the man told me that I would not even get a laboring job unless I shaved off my beard. Another clerk came over and said, 'We don't want no beatniks here, we give our jobs to Canadians.' "

Miss Ku stopped and sighed with the greatest sympathy. "The Guv wears a beard because he cannot shave, his jaw- bones have been smashed by the Japanese kicking him when a prisoner. I wish we could get out of Canada, or at least out of Ontario," Miss Ku added. I felt more sorry than I could say. I knew what it was to be persecuted for no valid reason. I got up, walked over to the Guv and told him of my sympathy. Miss Ku called after me, "Don't say anything to Buttercup about it, we don't want to disillusion her about Canada -- Oh! I forgot, she does not understand Cat!" The rest of the day the Guv was very quiet and had little to say to anyone. When we went to bed that night I sat by his head and purred to him until at last he fell asleep.

After breakfast of the following morning, the Guv called Miss Ku and said, "Hey, Ku, we are going to Dorwin Plaza to see Mrs. Durr's new shop. Coming?" "Ho-ly! Yessir, Guv!" said Miss Ku in some excitement. "How about you, Feef?" the Guv asked me. "Not for me, Guv, thank you,' I replied, "I will help Buttercup look after the place." While the Guv, Ma and Miss Ku visited Mrs. Durr's shop, Buttercup took an extra bath and I sat on the Guv's bed and thought and thought.

"Whoops!" yelled Miss Ku as she dashed up the stairs. "Say, Feef, she's got a very good place -- I can't stay I must have a bite to eat first." She dashed through the room, scattering the rugs, and into the kitchen. I leisurely jumped off the bed and picked a careful way out to her, 'carful' as I did not want to trip over one of the displaced rugs. "Yep! She sure has got a nice place!" said Miss Ku between mouthfuls, "She has Cards for all Occasions, Greetings Cards for when you enter prison, Commiseration Cards for when you are dope enough to enter Canada, and Sorrow Cards for when you get married. The Works, Everything. She has loads of the Guv's books, "The Third Eye", and "Doctor from Lhasa". YOU should go, Feef, it's just up Dougal, cross the railroad tracks, and all the shops on the right is or are Dorwin Plaza. The Guv will take you anytime. French books, too, Feef!" I smiled to myself, and the Guv chuckled behind me, "How can my Feef read when she is blind?" he asked. Miss Ku. "Ow!" she exclaimed in contrition, "I forgot the Old Biddy couldn't see!"

The Guv became ill. Very ill. We thought he was going to die, but somehow he managed to cling to life. One night as I was watching over him -- the others had long since gone to bed -- a Man from the Other Side of Death came and stood beside us. I was used to these Visitors, all cats are, but this was a very special Visitor indeed. The blind, as I have already told you, are not blind when it comes to things of the astral.

The astral form of the Guv left the world body and smiled across at the Visitor. The Guv, in the astral, was wearing the robe and vestments of a high Abbot of the Lamaistic Order. I purred fit to burst when the Visitor bent over me and tickled my chin and said, "What a very beautiful Friend you have here, Lobsang." The Guv trailed astral fingers idly through my fur, sending ecstatic shivers of delight through me, and replied, "Yes, she is one of the most loyal People upon the Earth." They discussed things and I shut my perceptions to telepathic thought, for one should NEVER steal the thoughts of others but only listen when so bidden. I did hear, though, "As we showed you in the crystal, we want you to write another book, to be called "The Rampa Story"."

The Guv looked sad, and the Visitor resumed, "What does it matter if people of the Earth do not believe? Perhaps they have not the capacity. Perhaps your books, in stimulating thought, will help them attain to such capacity. Even their own Christian Bible writes to the effect that unless they become as a little child, BELIEVING . . . !" The astral body of the Guv, in the shimmering golden Robes of the High Order, sighed, and said, "as you wish, having gone so far and suffered so much, it would be a pity to give up now."

Miss Ku pattered in. I saw her astral form jump straight out of her body with the shock of seeing te Shining Figures. "Chee!" she exclaimed, "do I ever feel a creep stealing in like this; will one bow be enough?" The Guv and the Visitor turned to her and laughed. "You are welcome anywhere, Lady Ku'ei," said the Visitor. "And so is my Old Granny Cat Feef!" said the Guv, putting his arms around me. The Guv was more fond of me, probably because he and I had suffered much through Life's hard blows. We, the Guv and I, had the strongest possible bonds between us. I liked it that way!

In the morning Ma and Buttercup came into the room tosee how the Guv was. "Well, you poor souls," he exclaimed, "I am going to write a fresh book." His remarks were met by groans. Ma and Buttercup went off to see Mrs. Durr and buy some paper, and other supplies. The Guv stayed in bed and I sat by him and looked after him. He was not well enough to write, but the book just HAD to be written. He started on it that day and sat in bed typewriter a-clatter.

"Twelve words to each line, twenty-five lines to each page, that is three hundred words to each page, and we will have about six thousand words, more or less, to the chapter," said the Guv. "Yaas, that's right enough, I guess," said Miss Ku.

"And don't forget that a paragraph should not be much more than a hundred words," she added, "or it will tire the customers!"

She turned away with a giggle and said, "YOU ought to write a book, Feef. Keep the Wolf from the Door. Buttercup can't or the Wolves would come flocking to her door if she unfolded her lurid tale." I smiled, Miss Ku was in high good humor, and that made me happy. The Guv reached out a hand and rubbed an ear. "Yes, you write a book, Feef, and I will type it for you," he said. "You must get on with 'The Rampa Story', Guv," I replied, "you have only typed the title so far." He laughed and rolled Miss Ku, who was trying to get on his lap in place of the typewriter, tail over head. "Come on, Feef!" she called as she sprang to her feet, "Come and play with me, let the Old Man play clackety with the typewriter."

Ma was talking to someone, I did not know who. "He is very ill," she said, "his life has been too hard. I do not know how he keeps on living." Miss Ku nudged me glumly, "Hope he doesn't croak, Feef," she said in a whisper, "he is quite useful to have around. I remember how gentle he was when my sister died. She was not even full grown, and she took ill and died in the Guv's arms. She was the spittin' image of you, Feef, the Fat Barmaid type. The Guv loved my sister Sue. Oh sure," she said, "you have your hooks on the Guv's heart all right. So have I, he admires my brains!" I jumped on the bed and went very close. He stopped typing to fondle me, he ALWAYS had time for us cats. "Don't die, Guv!" I said, "it would break the hearts of all of us." I rubbed my head against his arm as I got his telepathic message. Feeling more at ease, I felt my way to the foot of the bed and curled up.

Letters, letters, letters, were there NO jobs in Canada? Did they want only laborers? The Guv applied for job after job, but it seemed, as he said, that Canadians gave jobs only to Canadians or to those who had some political or union influence. Someone said that there were many jobs in more cultured, more civilized British Columbia, so the Guv decided to go there and see at first hand what the conditions were. He carefully conserved his strength and it was also decided that Buttercup would go as well in order to look after him. So the day came, and off they went to see if Vancouver conditions were better.

There is no joy when a Loved One is away, when the minutes are reluctant to drag on to the sorrowful hours, when there is an age of waiting, wondering. The house was dead, stale, even Ma moved quietly as if in a morgue. The light had gone from my soul, I felt the dank tendrils of fear come crowding in, telling me that he would not return, that he was ill, that -- ANYTHING that was fearsome and worrying. At night I crouched by his cold, empty bed after jumping up to make quite sure that it was not a nightmare. The blind live within themselves, and fears, to the blind, corrode and freeze one's soul.

Miss Ku played with forced gaiety. Ma looked after us, but her thoughts were elsewhere. There was a chill around which seeped inexorably through me. I sat on the telegram he had sent, and tried to gain comfort from it. This is a time which I must pass over quickly even in my writing. It will suffice to say that when the door opened and the Guv was back with me, I felt myself swell again with love; my ancient frame was almost ready to burst with joy, and I purred so long and loud that I almost got a sore throat.

I bumbled around, butting the Guv with my head, rubbing against everybody and everything. "Don't be such an ass, Feef," admonished Miss Ku, "one would think you were a young girl cat just out of the litter instead of an old woman great-great-great-grandmother cat; I'm shocked at your levity!" She sat primly, with her arms folded neatly in front of her. The Guv was telling Ma all about the trip, telling us too, if we listened instead of purring our heads off. Buttercup was not well, the trip and the different food had upset her, she was lying on her bed.

"We took off from Toronto Airport and were in Vancouver in four and a half hours. Not bad, considering the distance of a few thousand miles. We flew seven miles high above the Rockies."

"What are the Rockies, Miss Ku?" I asked in a whisper. "Lumps of big stones with snow on the top," she replied. "We found Vancouver very friendly, a nice place indeed," continued the Guv. "But there is much unemployment there. It is as different from Ontario as Heaven is from Hell. If ever we have the opportunity, that is where we will live."

Miss Ku rushed in, "I think Buttercup is dying," she gasped, "Shall I call the Undertaker?" The Guv and Ma went in to her bedroom, but poor Buttercup was only suffering from excitement and change of food and climate. The Guv was glad to assure Miss Ku that an Undertaker was NOT required!

"Look!" said the Guv to Ma, "I saw this in Vancouver and could not resist buying it. It is exactly like Mrs. Durr. I bought it for her." "Feef!" said Miss Ku in excitement, "he's got a small porcelain figure of a woman, she IS just like Mrs. Durr. Same color hair, same type of face, and Mrs. Durr also wears a crinoline. Gee!" exclaimed Miss Ku, "This will sure Knock her in the Old Kent Road!" I had to laugh, Miss Ku's slang was truly international; she even knew the worst of the French ones! As we lay in bed that night, with me beside the Guv, I felt my heart bursting with happiness. No longer did the crash of shunting trains seem threatening.

Now, as each railroad car bumped into the next, edging it forward, it seemed to say, "He's BACK, ha ha! He's BACK, ha ha!" I reached out and gently touched the Guv's hand with mine, and then fell asleep. For the next few weeks the Guv was very busy with "The Rampa Story". Special Visitors came from the world of the astral and talked long to him in the night. As the Guv tells in his books, there is no death, "death" is just the process of being reborn into another state of existence. It is all very complicated for a cat to explain. But it is so simple, so natural.

How is one to explain the process of taking successive breaths, or walking? How is one to explain the process of seeing? It is as difficult to explain all that as it is to explain just how there is no death. It is as easy to explain what life is as to explain what death is not. The Guv -- and cats -- can always see into the astral world and speak to the people of the astral. The time had come to think of another place in which to live. Windsor offered nothing. There was no possibility of employment, and the "Windsor scene" was dull and un-interesting. Few trees graced the area which was mainly industrial on a very small scale. The atmosphere was humid because of the great deposits of salt underlying the whole city.

As Miss Ku so aptly remarked, "Golly! What a cheesed-off dump Windsor is!" We looked at maps, and read books and at last we decided to move to a place on the Niagara Peninsula. Ma put an advertisement in newspapers in the hope of obtaining a suitable house. Replies came in, and most people with houses to rent seemed to think THEIR house was built of gold bricks, judging by the rents they asked.

We told our very nice Windsor Landlady's Cousin that we were leaving, and she was flatteringly sad. Now came the time of Great Cleaning. Buttercup's hobby is playing with a roaring vacuum cleaner, and this was a glorious excuse for her to get the thing screaming all day long. The Guv was confined to bed he had suffered from three attacks of coronary thrombosis in the past, and .had suffered from T.B. and other complaints. Writing "The Rampa Story" had taken much from him. Mrs. Durr came along and said to Ma, "I will drive you and the cats any time you wish. Perhaps Sheelagh can drive Dr. Rampa." We could always rely on Mrs. Durr for things like that; I knew that she would have the full support of Chuli.

We were going to take a furnished place and so wanted to sell our furniture which was almost new. No one wanted to buy it for cash; Canadians prefer to go to money lenders, whom they term

"Finance Companies" as that, they think, makes the affair rather more reputable. Having secured money from these money lenders, the Canadian usually buys gaudy things and pays so much a week. Miss Ku once told me that she had seen an advertisement "any car for ten dollars deposit" At last, the Guv and Ma heard of a very nice young man who was getting married, so they decided to give most of the furniture as a wedding present. Ma had previously made enquiries, and found that the cost of transferring the furniture would have been quite prohibitive. We were going to take a few specially cherished things and had made arrangements with a transport firm. Miss Ku and I were very glad that our Saw Horse was going. We had an old Saw Horse which we used as a Nail File and Jumping Platform. We also had an arrangement with the Guv whereby we would not scratch the furniture so long as we had our Nail File. Visitors sometimes stare when they see the Saw Horse among the furniture, but the Guv says "Never mind what people think, my cats come first!"

Down in the garden, Miss Ku called out loudly, "Hey! Across the Road Cat, come here!" Soon the cat came out of his back door, looked both ways for traffic, and then slipped across the road. He stood with his nose pressing against the wire fence waiting for Miss Ku to speak. "We are going away, Cat," she said, "Going away where the water flows fast. We are going to have a house with trees. You don't have trees, Cat!" "It must be wonderful to move around as you do, Lady Ku'ei!" remarked the Across the Road Cat. "I am going in now, but I will send you a telepathogram when we get to our new house."

The next morning the Moving Men came for the furniture which we were going to take. Things were carried down the stairs and loaded into a van which Miss Ku said was as big as a house. Soon the big doors closed with a slam, a powerful motor was started, and our belongings commenced their journey.

Now we had to sit on the floor like a lot of broody hens. I couldn't bump into anything now -- there was nothing that could get in the way! "Hey! Feef, we have not said goodbye to the attie," said Miss Ku. I jumped to my feet and rushed to join her at the upper stairs. Together we dashed up and climbed on the beams which kept the roof of the house on. Those beams were of walnut, from trees which used to be growing on the site when the Indians lived in the area. They were just BEAUTIFUL for sharpening claws; Miss Ku and I set to with a will to hone our claw edges to perfection, then we dashed through a small hole near the rising chimney where humans could not get. "Goodbye; spiders!" called Miss Ku, "now you can spin some more webs and you won't catch us!" We had a final roll in the dust beneath the floor- boards -- some had been left up when the electricians came -- and then we rushed down the stairs again almost out of breath.

A car drew up outside. Miss Ku jumped on to the window sill and yelled, "Come on, Ruth, LATE AGAIN AS USUAL! What's wrong with you, LEAD FEET?" Mrs. Durr came up the stairs and we all said good morning. Then everyone except the Guv carried little things down the stairs and put them into the cars. The Guv was very unwell and he had a sort of bed made up in the back of our big car. Buttercup was going to drive, as the Guv was ill, and they were going to do the journey in two stages. Ma, Mrs. Durr, Miss Ku and I were going to complete the two hundred and fifty something miles in one day. Soon all was ready for us to go. "Goodbye Guv," I called, "see you tomorrow." "Goodbye Feef," he replied, "Don't start worrying, everything will be all right." "O-kay!" said Miss Ku, "Let's roll!" Mrs. Durr did something with her feet and the car moved ahead. Over the railroad bridge, up past Walkerville Post Office, all the way up, leaving Windsor Airport on our left. I knew that district, but soon we were on fresh roads and I had to de- pend on Miss Ku for information.

"Saint Thomas is ahead!" yelled Miss Ku. Oh! I thought, did we have a crash, are we dead? How do we come to meet Saint

Thomas? "We are going to have some chow, Feef, as soon as we get clear of this joint," Miss Ku remarked. Then it dawned on me and I blushed at my stupidity; St. Thomas was a small city. In Canada a small village is a town and a bit bigger village is a city. Still, I suppose the French also have some peculiarities if I but knew them.

We drove for hours, and at last Miss Ku said, "The signs are telling me we are nearly there -- yes -- there is the Fort Erie Hotel. There is water ahead of us, Feef, the other end of the lake." "Are we there, Miss Ku?" I asked. "Good Grief no," she replied, "we have some more miles to go." I settled down again.

The car turned left, and sharp right. The engine slowed and stopped. Little crackling sounds came from the hot exhaust pipes. For a moment no one spoke, then Miss Ku said, "Well, here we are, Feef. Pick up your things." Ma and Mrs. Durr got out of the car and carried Miss Ku and me into the house. We were once again at a temporary home. Now I was anxious for the Guv to arrive, but that would not be until the morrow.

Chapter Twelve

"We must hurry, Feef," said Miss Ku, "the Guv and Buttercup arrive tomorrow and we must know every inch of the place before they get here. Follow me!" She turned and led the way into a room. "This is the Living Room," she re- marked; "Jump up here, it is three cats high, and then you are facing a window." She led me along, pointing out various items of interest. Then we wandered into the room which was going to be the Guv's bedroom and mine. "I can see the water through the trees, Feef," said Miss Ku. Just then a frightful clatter broke out beneath us, a roaring, grinding, clattering sound filled with many hisses. We jumped straight up in the air with fright, and coming down I missed the bed and fell on the floor. "Glory Be and Fifty Tomcats!" exclaimed Miss Ku, "WHAT WAS THAT?" Fortunately, Ma spoke to Mrs. Durr, "Oh! That will be the pump I expect, all the water is pumped from the lake."

We sat back at ease, there was nothing to worry about, I had memorized the noise. "There is a grille thing here, Feef," said Miss Ku, "Must be to let the water out if the house gets flooded or something." Startlingly there was a muffled roar beneath us, and hot air beat upon us like a giant's breath. We turned and fled to the safety beneath the bed and awaited results. "Aw gee!" said Miss Ku disgustedly, "There is nothing to it, that is just the heating blower. I thought first the biggest tomcat in all creation was coming after us."

"Feef!" Miss Ku gave me a nudge; I had been dozing. "Feef, there is a little wood outside. I expect the Old Man will let us play there when he gets on his hind legs again." It made me feel sad that the Guv was still on the road some- where and would not arrive until tomorrow. To distract my mind from such thoughts I rose to my feet and wandered around, feeling my way very carefully. From somewhere came a 'tap-tap' as a branch, blowing in the wind, knocked against the roof. The place was nothing wonderful, being quite 'run-down' but it would do for very temporary accommodation. It was not a place that we would want to call 'home,' we would not have lived there permanently even if it had been given to us.

That night we went to bed early. Mrs. Durr had to drive back to Windsor in the morning. Miss Ku and I had hoped that she was going to stay for a while, but as we thought about it we realized that her books would be lonely without her, and Mr. Chuli Durr was growing into a fine young Siamese Tomcat and would need attention. In the night the pump clattered and groaned, and the heating system wheezed and puffed. Outside the trees creaked and swished their leaves in the night wind which blew off the lake. Miss Ku crept close to me once during the night and whispered in a quavering voice, "Gee! Its a spooky place, Feef, with all these trees, and I just saw a great big spider looking at me!" The night seemed to last a very long time, when I was beginning to think it would never end I heard faint twitterings from birds in the trees as they made their food-finding plans for the day. Somewhere a squirrel scrabbled noisily beneath the window. I could sense that the day was upon us.

Ma stirred and reluctantly got up to face a new day, a day in which much had to be done in order to get the place clean. Miss Ku and I wandered around, trying to think of any places we had not already investigated. We knew there was a big basement underneath the house, but Ma had told us we could not go down there until the Guv came because there were pumps and things which whirred and buzzed and moved. We ambled idly into a front room and jumped on to a window sill. "Well I never! Did you ever?" exclaimed Miss Ku, "there is a thieving squirrel -- no -- HUNDREDS of them, eating our trees! " She tapped her foot with annoyance and, to distract her, I said, "What is it like out there, Miss Ku?" "Oh, quite a run-down place," she remarked, "trees need pruning, grounds need cleaning, house needs painting the usual run of things in these dumps which are rented. Read about it in the ads and you think you are going to a palace. See it, and you wonder how the heap will last for another winter."

The rest of the morning was very hard, furniture to be moved around and cleaning to be done and only Miss Ku and me there to tell Ma and Mrs. Durr how to do it. We were quite exhausted when Miss Ku looked out of the window and said, "The Guv and Buttercup have just driven in." "You are just in time to say goodbye!" said Mrs. Durr, "I must be getting back or I shall be in trouble!"

For the rest of the day we stayed in and worked. On the following day the weather was warm and sunny. The Guv said "Come on, cats, let us go into the garden!" He picked me up and put me across his shoulder. Miss Ku was already dancing with excitement at the door. We went out, and the Guv put me on the ground at the foot of a tree. "OW!" yelled Miss Ku, "The trees are so big!" "I used to climb trees like this, Miss Ku," I replied, "we had such trees in France." "Garth!" snarled the surly voice of Two Houses Back Cat, "You * * * * * foreign cats are no good nohow. Old blind cat there never climbed a tree in her life, only Canadian cats can climb -- and how!" He turned, and yelled derisively across to the Caretaker Cat from a local Institution. "Dese foreigners think we cats are hicks, they don't do no climbing!"

"Is that so Canadian Cat?" I responded, "Then let me show you that an old blind cat CAN climb!" I put my arms out stretched on the tree trunk and walked up as I used to do in France in the old bad days. I walked up about twenty five or thirty feet and then lay at full length along a branch.

Ma came rushing out full of concern, Buttercup came out as well, going "tsk! tsk! tsk!" They rushed round the house to where a ladder was stored. The Guv stood by the tree so that he could catch me if I fell. Ma and Buttercup came running up with the ladder, the Guv grabbed it and put it against the trunk. Slowly he climbed up, gently lifted me and put me across his shoulder. "Silly Old Woman Cat" he said mildly, "whoever heard of blind cats climbing trees!" I felt sorry, I could hear his heart thumping, and then I thought of his coronary thrombosis. Still, I HAD shown that stupid Canadian cat!

Miss Ku lay back and laughed and laughed and laughed. "Oh, Feef!" she exclaimed when she could control her mirth, "That was the funniest sight I've seen in years, you scared the acorns out of half a dozen squirrels -- they went leaping away like mad things. Two Houses Back Cat took off like lightning with One House Up Dog after him. Are you ever clever, Feef!" She was so amused that she lay on her back and rolled and rolled and rolled. "You ought to have your brains tested, Feef," said the Guv, "only you have no brains to test." Still, it made me feel good to know that a blind old French Siamese Cat could make Miss Ku laugh!

The Guv and Ma often took Miss Ku and me into the woods and let us play amid the trees. Knowing that cats are unpredictable, the Guv kept a ladder close at hand! The grounds swarmed with snakes, and Miss Ku was fascinated with them. I was always very careful as I was frightened of stepping on one. There was a Gentleman Ground Hog who lived in a hole in the ground near an old old tree. I spoke to him many times. Miss Ku said he used to sit at his front door and watch us as we took our exercise. Of course we kept our distance as we had not been introduced, but we had a high regard for him and he told us much about the place and about the local inhabitants of the trees and ground. "Watch out for the Raccoon," he said; "he plays a little rough if he is feeling cross, and he will knock the stuffing out of any dog. Well, I must go down and clean up!" He disappeared and Miss Ku said, "Gee! What in the name of Tarnation is a raccoon?" "I am afraid I cannot tell you, Miss Ku," I replied. She sat for a time, then scratching an ear reflectively, she remarked, "Ma collects those animal picture cards from the Tea Bag Boxes. I will have a look at them when we go in. Raccoon? Hmm!" We went in and Buttercup was dusting.

We always kept out of the way when she had a Dusting Mood on because there was always a danger that we would be swept up. All was dirt before her when she had a duster or vacuum cleaner in her hands. Miss Ku rummaged round and I heard things falling on to the floor. "What are you doing, Ku?" asked Buttercup a little crossly. "Come into the bed- room, Feef," said Miss Ku, "don't take any notice of Butter- cup, she has A Mood on because the Cleaner lead said 'ker-puff' and won't work."

There was a boat thing which the Guv had rented and one afternoon, when the sun was hot and high in the sky, he said, "Come on, let's take the cats on the lake." "Not me, Guv," I replied nervously, "Include me out!" "Oh come on, Feef, don't be such a sissy!" said the Guv. Ma carried Miss Ku and the Guv carried me. We went down the path to the lake and the Guv got the boat thing ready and held it tightly by a strong rope so that it would not escape. Ma and Miss Ku got on the thing and then the Guv lifted me in. There was some rocking and a splash or two and I felt us moving. "I won't start the motor," said the Guv, "the noise may be too much for them." We drifted along and Miss Ku sat in the front and sang "A seafaring cat am I." Unfortunately she had to break off to say "OW! I'm going to be seasick!"

The Guv pulled a piece of string and a motor roared at us and nearly frightened us into having kittens! The boat went fast and Miss Ku was so interested she forgot to be sick. She yelled at me, "We are twenty feet from America, Feef, this is Grand Island. This is Grand Boating, too!" Fortunately the sun got itself covered by a cloud and the Guv decided to take us home. I was

ı did not like to think of all that water around. I just
ɔ any sense in floating around in a thing that might
med to me that we had enough trouble without
more. We went home and then we had some tea.
Evenings were becoming shorter, so we all went to bed early.

Miss Ku and I sat on the window sill in the Guv's bed- room.
Outside there were all the sounds of the night. Beneath the
floorboards a field mouse said that it must get in some more
food for the coming winter. Suddenly Miss Ku crouched low and
growled deep in her throat. "Glory Be!" she exclaimed, "there is a
huge cat in a striped football jersey!" A very pleasant telepathic
voice broke in, "And are you the foreign Lady Cats that I have
heard about?" "Sure are, Bud," replied Miss Ku, "What in Heck
are you?" The Voice came again and there was a suspicion of a
chuckle in it, "I am Raku the Raccoon, I live here and keep the
night free of prowling dogs." "Pleased to meet you," replied Miss
Ku, "particularly as there is thick-plate glass between us!" "Oh!
You'd be quite safe with me," answered Raku the Raccoon, "I
always respect the interests of tenants. Now I must get about my
business."

"Miss Ku," I said, "He seems to be a very pleasant, gentleman,
what does he look like?" She thought for a moment then settled
down to wash as she replied, "Well, he looks like a whacking
great tomcat, biggest tomcat you ever saw. Bigger than many
dogs. Stripes all along his tail as if he had got bars of wet paint
from some cage. And his claws . . . !" She paused for emphasis,
and then added, "He's got claws like the thing Buttercup uses to
rake up the leaves. Oh! A VERY pleasant gentleman -- if one
keeps the right side of him, and the right side is with a brick
wall in between." The Voice came again, "Hey! Before I forget, feel
free to use the woods as if you owned the place, you will be very
welcome!" "I am sure we are most honored," I replied, "I will ask
Ma to invite you to tea sometime." "Well!" exclaimed Miss Ku,
"Guess I must hit the sack. Busy day tomorrow, the Guv is

taking me to Ridgeway -- I have some shopping to do." She wandered off to sleep beside Ma.

The weather was rapidly becoming colder. Leaves were falling with a continuous dry rustle, and the squirrels, who had been idle through the false warmth of the autumn, were rooting frantically through the piles of leaves in search of acorns. Buttercup raked leaves, talked leaves, and smelled of leaves. Still the leaves came down in endless profusion.

The smoke of burning leaves rose to the heavens from all the houses in the district and from the great stretches of parkland. The air became colder, now only the Guv went out without his coat. Buttercup wrapped up -- as Miss Ku said -- as if she were at a particularly cold North Pole. One morning we awakened to find snow driving across the lake, piling up in front of the house, and making the roads impassable. With tremendous roars and clatters the snow ploughs came out, their scraper blades slithering and juddering along the icy surface of the road.

After the snow, came the freeze-up. The lake froze, a nearby creek became a solid mass of ice. Crazy fishermen came with special tools and cut holes in the several-feet- thick ice so that they could sit and shiver and pretend to catch fish. Morning after morning the roads were snowed up and traffic was halted. Great storms raged and howled around the house. One night the water pump stopped. The Guv got out of bed at two in the morning and went down to the lake carrying a great iron bar and a heavy hammer. Ma got up and put on the kettle for tea. I could hear hammering and the sound of breaking ice. "Miss Ku," I asked, "What is it all about?" "If the Guv can't break up the ice around the water intake we shall have no water for the winter. Y'see, Feef, it is so cold that the lake has frozen. The Old Man has gone to dig out the ice and then we shall keep a tap slightly on." I shuddered, this Canada seemed to be a cold, cruel country, with no civilized amenities such as one would have in Europe.

With the coming of the cold, Ma put out food every night for the wild creatures who otherwise would have died of starvation. Mister the Raccoon was very grateful and came to our window every night. Mister the Canadian Badger came as well, but the most amusing episode was provided by Mouse Rouse! Buttercup was doing some washing in the basement one day when a very pleasant, well-spoken mouse came and sat on her foot. (Miss Ku says it was a lemming, but mouse is good enough for me.) This Mouse formed a firm attachment for Buttercup and she seemed to be equally attached to him. After the monkey episode nothing at all surprised us about Buttercup. "We must remember our manners, Feef, and not eat the fellow," said Miss Ku. Butter- cup and Mouse Rouse had many pleasant moments together in the basement. Miss Ku and I assured him that we would not harm him, so he took no notice of us but just mooned about after Buttercup. It was MOST touching!

The winter gave way to spring and we were glad to leave that place and move to another nearer the shops. There was still no work available for the Guv. In desperation he wrote to the Prime Minister of Canada, to the Minister of Im- migration, and to the Minister of Labor. Not one of them seemed to care in the slightest; these Ministers appeared to be even worse than those in other countries. I suppose that it is because Canada is so uncultured, so unfriendly. Now we live in hopes of making enough money to get OUT of Canada!

I sat in the window of our new Apartment and had a friendly chat with the Cat who ran a Motel. I told him of our adventures. "Aw, Feef!" said Miss Ku, "You should write a book!" I turned it over in my mind, and in the stillness of the night, when both of us were awake, I discussed it with the Guv. "Guv!" I said, "Do you think I could write a book?"

"Sure you could, Feef," he replied, "You are a very intelligent Old Granny Cat." "But I can't type," I protested,

"Then you shall dictate it to me and I will type it for you, Feef," he said. In the morning we sat down together. He opened the typewriter, the grey Olympia which already has typed "The Third Eye", "Doctor from Lhasa", and "The Rampa Story". Opened the typewriter, and said, "Come on, Feef, start dictating!" So, with his encouragement, and with Miss Ku to help me, I have at last finished this book. Do you like it?

THE END

INNER LIGHT PUBLICATIONS
BOX 753
NEW BRUNSWICK, N.J. 08903